Between East and West

EUROPEAN PERSPECTIVES

A Series in Social Thought and Cultural Criticism
Lawrence D. Kritzman, Editor

European Perspectives presents outstanding books by leading
European thinkers. With both classic and contemporary works,
the series aims to shape the major intellectual controversies of
our day and to facilitate the tasks of historical understanding.

For a complete list of books in the series, see pages 149–151

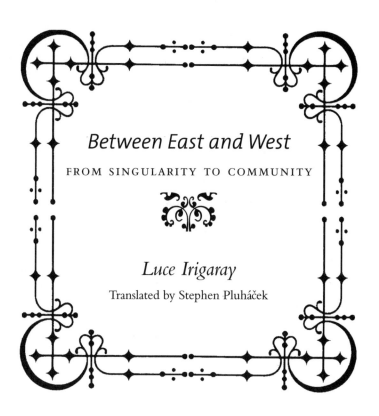

Between East and West

FROM SINGULARITY TO COMMUNITY

Luce Irigaray

Translated by Stephen Pluháček

COLUMBIA UNIVERSITY PRESS

NEW YORK

Columbia University Press
Publishers Since 1893
New York   Chichester, West Sussex

Translation copyright © 2002 Columbia University Press
Entre Orient et Occident © 1999 Editions Grasset et Fasquelle
All rights reserved

Columbia University Press wishes to express its appreciation
for assistance given by the government of France through the
Ministère de la Culture in the preparation of this translation.

Library of Congress Cataloging-in-Publication Data
Irigaray, Luce.
[Entre Orient et Occident. English]
Between East and West : from singularity to community /
Luce Irigaray ; translated by Stephen Pluháček.
p. cm. — (European perspectives)
Includes bibliographical references (p.).
ISBN 0–231–11934–8 (cloth : alk. paper)
ISBN 0–231–11935–6 (pbk. : alk. paper)
1. Feminist theory. 2. Man-woman relationships.
3. Prānayāma. 4. East and West.
I. Title. II. Series.
HQ1190 .174713   2002
305.42'01—dc21   2001042240

Casebound editions of Columbia University Press books
are printed on permanent and durable acid-free paper.

Printed in the United States of America
Designed by Audrey Smith

C 10 9 8 7 6 5 4 3 2 1
P 10 9 8 7 6 5 4 3 2

CONTENTS

Humanity seems past. Philosophies and religions are in a period of taking stock. The dominant discipline in the human sciences is now history. Sociology, which shares the spotlight with it, is dedicated to the description of what already exists. We should be what apparently we are, what we have already shown of ourselves. As for the rest, our becoming would be prescribed by our genes, or by what has already been deciphered of them. Our growth is to have stopped one day. We are to have become at best objects of study. Like the whole living world, destroyed little by little by the exploration-exploitation of what it is instead of cultivating what it could become.

Wanting to invent a new future would be pure utopia, claim the exhausted human beings. Let us remain in the past. Let us celebrate the dead. Let us forget the living. Supposing that any remain . . . Because that which does not grow wastes away.

How long have we been declining? And how to go against the current? To stop the exploitation, in particular through a simple inventory, of the human and of his or her environment? How to return to where death has taken place because of the cessation of becoming, mistaking what we are? How to renew a cultivation of life, and recover our energy, the path of our growth? *Between East and West* proposes or recalls some places starting from which the work of our human becoming may resume.

Unlike the plant, the human being is a living being without fixed roots. One that walks, is mobile. One that also moves in spirit. Differently than the animal? In space and in time, the human being moves. That makes possible acquiring material and spiritual food, but also going astray, sometimes at the risk of existence. What, then, can safeguard existence in a living being that is partly nomadic in body and spirit? The breath. Breath is the source and food of natural and spiritual life for the human being. To cultivate life comes down to preserving and educating breathing, the origin of an autonomous existence, but also of the soul, understood in its original sense, as living.

The human being is made of matter but also of breath. Thanks to a mastery of breath, a surplus of life can be brought to the body, modifying its metabolism, its nature, its inertia. The human being can transfigure it, transubstantiate it, overcome a part of its heaviness. Western man has generally neglected, even forgotten, this ability. Separating body and spirit, he has valorized the one, as the result of a disincarnated speech, making of the other a vehicle, necessary but cumbersome, during existence said to be earthly. The spiritualization of the body and of the senses has not yet appeared to him as a specifically human task thanks to which he may transcend a material status, overcome suffering, solitude, illness, and, in a way, death. A cultivation of breathing, of energy maintains life and health better than abandoning a body-cadaver-animal to medical science and its diverse types of operations. Progress in the mastery of breathing, of the physical and psychic metabolism, also results in meaning that advancing in age does not necessarily equal a decline, as we generally think. Which leads us to spurn the wisdom, among other things the carnal wisdom, of elders and their teaching.

Western man has above all failed to recognize and has neglected that which, it seems to me, should characterize his species: the ability to enter into relation with the other without reducing this relation to the satisfaction of instincts, of needs. The Western subject has come to a standstill at a moment in his journey. He has tried to identify himself through differentiation from the mother, whom he assimilates to nature. A good many strategies—philosophical, religious, scientific—find their cause and their inspiration in this often unconscious and blind process. In this effort of differentiation, man has undervalued his proper nature and has passed to another type of indifferentiation: that with his peers, his social group, his civilization. Hence the adherence to a natural or spiritual family, to a nation, to a tradition that prevents him from welcoming the other, the different, he or she who remains foreign to him. Hence also the loss of the near in the proper, of proximity in property.

The teaching of nature, in a sense, was more wise. Humanity is made up of two different human beings. In the cultivation of their relation can be found the key to the flourishing of the species. This cultivation, in fact, leads each person to individualize himself or herself in comparison to what is lived as primitive indifferentiation, especially on the part of man. In the respect for the two, the remedy for a relapse into the indifferentiation of the group, including the familial group, is also discovered. As for sexual difference, in which attraction originates, it offers the basis for a specifically human behavior. Instead of the male-female relation being determined by the immediacy of instinct, the transformation of instinct into desire could mark the passage to humanity as such. From then on the attraction between the sexes becomes a source of energy and creation that is not only natural but also cultural, resulting from the will and the freedom of two human beings.

The ability to enter into relation with one (man or woman) who is other than oneself in the respect of difference(s) is, according to me, what permits the constitution of a properly human subjectivity. Neither language as a tool of appropriation and information nor the capacity to control what is and efficiency in the intervention upon the real are specific to human being. But the negative, the step back, listening and silence, the necessary alternation of doing and letting be, toward self and other, in the relation to a different subject are perhaps its irreducible sign.

yes

On this way, we have not advanced very far. It holds for us sources of energy, of speech and wisdom that we still do not know. It represents without any doubt a place starting from which to resume and to pursue human becoming. Not as the act and according to the will of one subject alone, but beginning from the horizon opened by the recognition of the existence of two different subjects who work toward the construction of bridges between them while safeguarding their own singularity.

I thank Columbia University Press for passing on to Anglophone readers these suggestions on the way to get out of the peril in which humanity as such finds itself today. The task of thinking is too little considered in our time. And the publishing world does not sufficiently interpret, in my opinion, the risk that it itself runs as being tied to scorn for the thinker. It is not purely economic or technical strategies, nor submission to the ultimate imperatives of an advertising and media culture that will restore to the world of publishing the status that it must assume in society. It is rather the concern for awakening and maintaining in the reader the taste for thinking as a vital dimension for humanity and its blossoming. It is also the sense of responsibility toward citizens who, through exposure to thinkers, can safeguard their critical sense and their freedom from every form of totalitarianism, latent and masked as it is. To each citizen of a democratic regime falls the task of thinking in order to resist all manipulation of opinion and to consciously determine his or her civic and cultural decisions.

I thank Stephen Pluháček for the way in which he carried out the translation of *Between East and West*. He gave time for listening to thought. He prepared a receptiveness for its welcoming. His work does not represent a simple passage from one language to another, with the loss of meaning and of style that often results. It bears witness to an exchange between thinkers, the place where speech is generated, comes to light, and is put to the test. This exchange is all the more notable and touching in that it unfolds between a man and a woman. A man who, like at the origin of our Western culture—as certain of the so-called pre-Socratic philosophers testify—agreed to set about listening to her: nature, woman, divinity, and tried to make her message understood without appropriating it in a discourse in the masculine. Without doubt it is to this moment of the constitution of the Western subject that we must return in order to remember the forgetting of her—and Her—and to strive to undertake a dialogue between us, woman and man, women and men, that assures memory and reveals little by little the fecundity of our double truth—natural, human, divine. I thank Stephen Pluháček for having had the intelligence and the humility necessary for beginning to carry out this return, not only in the context of a solitary or magisterial discourse of one's own, but in the effective reality of a dialogue. I also thank Heidi Bostic, his companion, for having supported him in this work.

I would also like to acknowledge Alessandro Angelini, who, even before *Between East and West* had found an English-language publisher and an official translator, had agreed to reread with me a part of "The Way of Breath" that I had translated for a presentation in London and had then pursued alone the translation of several chapters of the book. Perhaps we will one day have the opportunity to again undertake such a collaboration starting from a more literary text?

Stephen Pluháček, Heidi Bostic, and Alessandro Angelini participated in seminars that I held in Paris either in the context of the CNRS (Centre National de la Recherche Scientifique) or in that of a Parisian program of Wesleyan University. I am grateful to them for ensuring a continuity to their listening and to our dialogues. I hope that they will find in this faithfulness to thought and to friendship a path for becoming themselves and for accomplishing the task that falls to them, with earnestness and joy.

Paris, March 2001

Between East and West

Introduction

"There is much that is strange, but nothing that surpasses man in strangeness" (Sophocles, *Antigone*, vv. 332–333).

To be sure, our age has much that is uncanny, but less than man himself, however. What is uncanny about it comes from what is uncanny about *him*, and all the interpretations of our ill-being, all the remedies that are proposed or provided are powerless to account for the cause of the worrying if they do not question what man has been for centuries: they are too partial and superficial and do not get back to the source from which the danger is born. All the interpretations, like all the remedies, come, then, like man himself to nothing. And death, of each and of all, seems the only thing that resists man's destructive power.

Has he not, in fact, exhausted the earth, prevailed by his cunning over the wild animal, over the birds and the fishes, subjected to his work the horse and the ox, invented the all-comprehending through speech, and also the government of cities and the victory over cosmic storms? Has he not dominated all, or almost all, by his cleverness, only to arrive at nothing? And, surveying from on high the world, his world, does he not find himself finally excluded from it?

Through love of audacity, of challenge, forcing his way between heaven and earth, has he not brought both to ruin? Has he not confused what is and what is not, exercising his know-how, building and constructing before asking what is, what he himself is? Advancing from illusion to illusion without securing his knowledge of the real, beginning with the reality that he himself is?

"May such a man never frequent my hearth; may my mind never share the presumption of him who does this" (Sophocles, *Antigone*, vv. 373–375).

Thus spoke the chorus around twenty-five hundred years ago, at the beginning of the tragedy *Antigone* by Sophocles.

We, women and men of today, can make such words ours and meditate on them in order to quit deluding ourselves any longer. The economic crisis of our time, to give but one example that fascinates us about our ill-being, is only a symptom of what man himself has been for centuries.

To resolve the economic problem without treating its cause amounts to man going a little further into exile from himself, from his world, and hastening a little more quickly his ruin, that of the human species, that of the planet.

To be sure, there is no lack of demagogues to push everyone away from a necessary realization, to use the economic malaise itself with the aim of deluding everyone still further about their innocence and irresponsibility, to lure everyone even more, inside an identical horizon or project, toward impossible solutions but probable disasters.

And do not think that I am amusing myself here by elaborating beautiful metaphors in order to support my own utopia. I am speaking here of real things. But who still has ears to perceive something of the real?

How therefore to reopen the horizon of a world that has become foreign to the one who constructed it and that represents a danger for all?

Two gestures appear necessary: to reground singular identity and to reground community constitution.   yes

Perhaps because I am a woman, I do not utter such words from above or from outside a world that I built by always distancing myself from myself and from the pre-given universe that surrounds me. They are rather born from a quest for myself, for the world, for the other, beyond illusions, beyond lies.

Perhaps because I am a woman, I have perceived and lived the danger more quickly and otherwise; which earned me some years ago, and still today, suspicions of all sorts. But I love life, and I have searched for solutions in order to defend it, to cultivate it: for me and in itself.

These solutions will appear too modest to some, too ambitious to others. They are looking to return to this side of artifices that have stolen me from myself, from the world, from the relation with the other, with others. They want to transform the survival that imposes itself upon me in uncovering the very source of life, both individual and collective.

To deconstruct, certainly, but that already represents a luxury for whoever has not built a world. And who or what supplies the energy for such a gesture? Would it be inspired by hatred? Of whom or of what? Of all, of everyone, and of oneself? Does such an operation really go beyond the existing logic, notably beyond its opposition between love and hate, whose importance in the construction of our horizon was signaled by Empedocles? Does not deconstruction, including through its recourse to innumerable linguistic ruses, remain trapped in a secular manner of know-how, and does it not imprison there reason itself, to the point of leading it to a nihilistic madness as the ultimate Promethean gesture? Would it not also be too mental, too exclusively mental, wanting to ignore that the sensible-intelligible and corporeal-spiritual dichotomies are one of the reasons for the disturbing character of man and of his world? And does not the technical cleverness of the deconstructor risk accelerating, without possible check or alternative, a process that appears henceforth almost inevitable?

To break chains, to reopen prisons, to unveil lies and illusions: yes. But how to do this without starting again from the elemental of life itself and, in particular, from the first and last gesture of natural and spiritual life: to breathe by oneself?

To discover that I can live in an autonomous manner, that no one is absolutely necessary for me, that I do not need to invent mothers or fathers for myself in order to subsist. To breathe by myself allows me also to move away from a sociocultural placenta. Thus I can begin to be born, to no longer live from the breath of anyone, as the fetus does in the womb of its mother and as man often does inside a given historical horizon. To be born to my life. To be born also to a certain cultural naïveté: to not need to break in order to discover or rediscover what is, what is beautiful, what is true. To perceive it through a personal renaissance.

Here again, it is not a question of being satisfied with just words. In any case, Western culture had not taught me the way of what I thus began to test by necessity and in a solitary manner. Like some recent philosophers of the West, I needed to turn myself toward the East in order to find guides and basic principles of method. I did this differently than the Western masters. I did not claim to incorporate the knowledge of Eastern masters in my knowledge, nor even to pass from their words to my words. This type of transmission appeared to me to have become obsolete. I followed the teaching of masters for whom a daily practice—in fact, yoga—was what could help awaken or reawaken and discover words and gestures carrying another meaning, another light, another rationality.

If learning again to breathe, naively at first and then with the aid of masters from the East, or trained in the East, helped me at first to continue to live and continues to have this meaning, little by little this allowed me to glimpse the existence of another life, not in the beyond but here below. It was possible to live altogether otherwise than I had been taught, than what I could imagine.

This "otherwise" has nothing in common with the discovery of some unconscious. To tell the truth, my first encounter with a yoga teacher, which was rather conflictual, took place around the possibility of everything becoming conscious, as he declared to his students. As a psychoanalyst, I

made him understand his naïveté. I could not see my own!
And no more the fact that we were speaking starting from
two different horizons. The practice of respiration, the practice of diverse kinds of breathing certainly reduces the dark-
ness or the shadows of Western consciousness. But above all
it constitutes the mental in a different way. It grants more
attention to the education of the body, of the senses. It
reverses in a way the essential and the superfluous. We Westerners believe that the essential part of culture resides in
words, in texts, or perhaps in works of art, and that physical
exercise should help us to dedicate ourselves to this essential.
For the masters of the East, the body itself can become spirit
through the cultivation of breathing. Without doubt, at the
origin of our tradition—for Aristotle, for example, and still
more for Empedocles—the soul still seems related to the
breath, to air. But the link between the two was then forgotten, particularly in philosophy. The soul, or what takes its
place, has become the effect of conceptualizations and of
representations and not the result of a practice of breathing.
The misunderstandings are so profound, proportional to historical forgetting and repressions, that bridges between the
traditions are difficult to restore.

I will try to give an example of this difficulty drawn from
Schopenhauer's idea of the genius of the species. This West-

ern philosopher, concerned with Indian culture, asserts nevertheless that the life of man is dominated by a blind passion, that of reproducing himself. Now if the Indians take care to assure the perpetuation of life, if they generally give birth to two children in order to fulfill their duty toward human existence, they do not, for all that, bear witness to a passion for reproduction. They love and cultivate life, but not in the manner of a pressing need to reproduce their own species. Their objective is rather to spiritualize their body and nature, as micro- and macrocosm, to make them pass, beginning now and here below, from the mortal to the immortal, from the imperfect to the perfect. The way taken is generally the cultivation of respiration and the renunciation of investing in something partial, in any object, that brings grief and heartbreak to the self. Unlike the contempt for individuation, which results from Schopenhauer's theory, the Hindu tries to bring his incarnation to the point of perfection in order to avoid reincarnation, especially in a less accomplished form.

An Eastern culture often corresponds to becoming cultivated, to becoming spiritual through the practice of breathing. In this becoming the body is not separated off from the mental, nor is consciousness the domination of nature by a clever know-how. It is a progressive awakening for the entire being through the channeling of breath from centers of elemental vitality to more spiritual centers: of the heart, of speech, of thought. This requires time! Often an entire life-time, a time that must remain in harmony with the rhythm of life in general, that of the universe and that of other living beings, which the candidate to the spiritual must respect, and even try to aid if such is their wish.

Spiritual progress is therefore not separated off from the body nor from desire, but these are gradually educated to renounce what harms them. To be sure, it is not a matter of renouncing for the sake of renouncing, but of renouncing what impedes access to bliss in this life. Asceticism is not there-fore privative as it has too often been in the West. It is a limi-tation, accepted and willed, in order to progress toward happi-ness. Such is the case with sexuality for example. Chastity is not presented as a good in itself, and the candidate for monas-ticism is often invited to first prove himself on the sexual plane. The gods of India, moreover, generally appear as a cou-ple: man and woman creating the universe through their familiarity with certain elements, through their love as well, and they destroy it through their passion. We are far from the philosophico-religious representations that have characterized the West for several millennia.

To go back and meditate starting from practices and texts of Eastern cultures, especially pre-Aryan aboriginal ones, can show us a way to carry on our History. It has been like this for me. And, for some years, I have noted with pleasure that I am not the only one to take an interest in these cultures! Unfortunately, Westerners retain above all their post-Aryan aspects, which are less disorienting for them than the more feminine aboriginal cultures. Even the teachers of yoga trained in India forget the importance of sexual difference in the culture that they pass on. Only the old masters insist on this dimension of their tradition, which is present, moreover, in the texts. Alas, the current practice draws inspiration a little too much from what is most disturbing about the West: the cleverness of technique, the domination of nature, the forgetting of the fundamental character of the difference of the sexes.

If I have learned from my yoga teachers the importance of breathing in order to survive, to cure certain ills, and to attain detachment and autonomy, I have not received from them, neither male nor female, any information about a sexuation of breathing or of energy, about its usefulness in the respect and love of self or of other. I had to invent and pursue this course alone: by practicing, by listening (to myself), by reading, by awakening myself, by creating links with the West, including to cure certain sufferings. What I live and think today is woven between two traditions, provided that there really are two and that it is not rather a matter of a development of human consciousness, more or less present or forgotten. In the chapter "Eastern Teachings" I have tried to say what yoga taught me (or recalled to me) and what this tradition has not (yet?) conveyed to me.

Since the writing of that text, I have progressed, at least I hope so . . . Particularly through responding to the questions that I asked myself or that were asked of me. In "The Way of Breath," I attempted to say how the practice of respiration, of breathing, is not neuter, and how woman and man breathe and use their breath in a specific manner: the one keeping it more inside, notably to share it, the other employing it almost exclusively to make, to construct outside the self. I have proposed some explanations for the attraction that man feels for woman, starting from this greater interiority of the breath, and made some suggestions about the way to cultivate desire without giving up living it carnally.

This union between the sexes, beyond any already established representation, corresponds to the most deconstructive gesture that can exist, in a sense. But it carries out at the same time, and in the same gesture, a possible refoundation at the level of the least constructed, at the most intimate level of human being itself and of its living relations with the pre-given world that surrounds it: nature, other living beings.

Furthermore, does not to succeed in sharing this first and ultimate gesture of life, natural and spiritual, correspond to the source or the bridge from which to rethink both singularity and community?

To respect my life, the life of the universe, the life of the other, is this not the first gesture of a culture escaping from what is uncanny, a culture where spirit is constituted without dominating nature or moving away from it in order to appropriate it, whether nature be the pre-given environment, one's own body, or that of other living beings? Is this not to substitute for our traditional upbringing a culture where consciousness awakens thanks to the progressive spiritualization of the body by the breath, the most familiar, the most originary becoming the most cultivated, the ultimate, without, for all that, leaving the pre-given world in order to intensify what is disturbing about it by a still greater disturbance but in seeking, on the contrary, to render what is uncanny familiar?

And, if this gesture is carried out by two, does it not represent a possible refoundation of the "us," on this side and beyond differences but thanks to these very differences? This gesture, a possible refoundation of the subjectivity of man, of woman, and of their relation that is foundational for community, also permits the coexistence, without cultural pregiven, of diverse traditions with which today we have to compose a society. Breath is, indeed, what can be shared by all men and by all women on this side and beyond differences of culture. It demands just one thing: the respect of the natural and spiritual life of the self and of the other.   yes

How to articulate singularity and community? This question cuts across that of the relations between East and West in a way that is complex and, according to me, unfulfilled.

The elements that separate the two traditions are multiple. There enters into it an estrangement from the local site, from the living ties with the plant kingdom, the animals, the   yes humans, and the gods that are part of this local site. Whereas the pre-given place, the birthplace, served as second mother, sheltering with its landscape, nourishing with its fruits, comforting with its surroundings and with its customs, the wrenching away from the place of birth forced the invention of other recourses: the hunt, the tools necessary to feed and to shelter oneself and equally to make war. Nomads conquer their territory against the familiarity of the first site, against the sedentary, against the more maternal, more feminine values. They create a culture of between-men, who are enemies or accomplices, for which the divinity is instead patriarchal, God-the-Father, everywhere present and never there, whom one follows, who accompanies you, who censures you and assists you, who imposes his laws on wandering peoples use escaping from the measures of a more natural life.

These migrations that changed individual and collective

identity have intervened between the Asiatic aboriginal traditions and our Western cultures. Whereas nature, proximity, dialogue and oral transmission, and local customs served as norms for the community, the social grouping, property, and written codes organize it in a more formal manner with a loss of individual consistency and of relations between human beings. To be sure a link exists, but it is ruled by law and a certain distribution of goods. The common is defined by property and not proximity. Community is no longer constituted starting from intimate relations of kinship, from closeness with others, but from the outside, starting from rules, from goods, from borders that are more or less foreign to the subject(s).

An enclave resists this conception of the community: the family. In it certain features of aboriginal archaic cultures live on: familiarity, a settled way of life, oral sharing, natural and common law. The State, it is true, strives to substitute its norms here: demanding children, labor, goods, the submission of singularity to an abstract and artificial conception of the individual. The family, like woman, moreover, is simultaneously overvalorized and devalorized, colonized. It is subjected to values that are foreign to it and that, little by little, destroy it. Not without failing to recognize what constitutes it, the patriarchal foundations, which have undermined it, claim henceforth to restore it by exercising a certain mastery over it, by imposing a certain power over it. One may as well end up in an empty house!

In fact, it is instead a matter of thinking and of restoring certain relations between feminine aboriginal cultures and patriarchalized Indo-European cultures, aiming not toward a reversal of power but a possible coexistence of perspectives, of subjectivities, of worlds, of cultures. This implies passing beyond predominantly *genealogical* traditions, be they matriarchal or patriarchal, that are today in opposition, toward the constitution of *horizontal* relations between the sexes.

Drawing inspiration from pre-Aryan civilizations, I attempted to find the places of articulation between man and woman, and even between all men and all women, in particular through breathing. To pass to the level of Western community requires other methods. Besides the difficulty of such a collective constitution, to remain at the level of breathing would risk favoring social organizations where the person is alienated and even disappears in the group. Moreover, the Eastern traditions themselves are multiple at present, and the Asiatic aboriginal and Indo-European contributions live together there without real articulation between them. Therefore it is not a question of simply reversing History but of examining its stratifications and successive layers in order to strive toward its construction.

yes

That is the way of the Hegelian dialectic, a method unsurpassed in a sense, but one that lets its own aporias appear in the impossibility of discovering or constructing modalities of spirit that respect feminine ethical values and masculine cultural values. In order not to sacrifice the piety of Antigone to the power of Creon, a double dialectic is necessary, rather than a universalization that always draws away from the real in the name of abstract or so-called objective values. It does not help to organize values in a hierarchy starting out from the natural pre-given toward more and more artificially fabricated ideals. It is important to redialecticize the relations between nature and culture with respect for the realities that compose the pre-given world: that of the macrocosm and that of living beings, for whom sexual difference is an unavoidable natural and cultural reality.

Certain historical factors might seem more important to us than treating the difference of the sexes: those tied to the migrations of our age, for example. Now these migrations risk carrying us off toward an increasingly disturbing neutralization and phantomization of the environment and of the individual, accompanied by an authoritarian guardianship that surrounds or integrates the multiple and the foreigner. The recent paternalist era claims to be plural, but it is a plural often remaining inside the closure of the patriarchal world. Furthermore, the human spirit needs to be able to gather together, to unify, in order to become while remaining itself and capable of fidelity to the other; it also has need of familiarity. It is therefore indispensable to discover a new universe of the *one* and of the *familiar*. Sexual difference can provide us with this.

To be sure, the *one* is carried then from the individual to the *relation between two*. The community will be composed of relations-between and not of one + one + one ... juxtaposed and gathered together by exterior and more or less artificial laws.

The fundamental relation will be constituted of and by two who are different, each irreducible to the other but united by a natural attraction that it is fitting to cultivate by keeping it close to familiarity, or more exactly by making it familiar. Sexual attraction is in effect foreign, and often its foreignness finds itself restricted by the nostalgia for, or the regression to, the genealogical dimension. The familiar in this case is not spiritualized as such, not elevated to the level of self-consciousness, and a hierarchical relation dominates the relation to the other. Too natural and too cultural, the genealogical dimension does not permit this restructuring of the relations between nature and culture that we need.

Sexual difference can bring us there and, thanks to it, diverse sorts or forms of others may be approached without renouncing a becoming of one's own.

What is at stake regarding the *proper* then changes accent. We do not have to make the world, including the other who inhabits it, our own, but we have to discover what is proper to us and cultivate it in order to be able to greet as different, but sometimes familiar, that which and those who surround us.

The near [*proche*] calls for difference. If the other or I lack our proper borders, we cannot approach one another. We each appropriate the other to the point of forgetting the man or the woman who is close to us.

The customs of the maternal world are generally ruled by proximity, but a proximity unthought as such. The patriarchal world, on the other hand, is based on property, but the proper of man remains foreign to it. It falls to each of these worlds to acknowledge a being proper to it and to cultivate it. Which supposes accepting the distancing from, even the rupture of, the first links, but in order to recognize and to cultivate their familiarity, including beyond the birthplace and the family of origin.

Between human being and nature, another proximity can reveal itself and work itself out with sexual difference as the mediation. By drawing away from the first given familiarity, man and woman can perceive and cultivate, by the work of love and desire, that which exists between them. In this way the horizon of a new foundation of the family and of the community opens a little, which represents progress in the development of human consciousness.

Antigone and Hölderlin will be able to renounce here nostalgias that are still too simple, immediate and egological, in order to try to build spiritual links between their singularities. And that could become the cradle of their renaissance.

The Time of Life

I will situate these questions under the sign or the oracle of opening, thus of egological nonclosure, of renunciation of narcissistic self-importance, the first condition of listening and of speaking that the tradition of India taught me.

According to this tradition, no theory or practice is ever completed. Both are always evolving. The task is to try to connect the here and now of today, this present moment of our life, to the reality of yesterday and that of tomorrow. It is useless therefore to do too much in order to immortalize the whole immediately. It is impossible. On the other hand, it is a matter of doing enough to attempt to pass from the present reality to immortality or eternity.

Moreover, I do not know the exact historical date of this present moment, its material or spiritual birthdate; I do not know its age. This imprecision regarding the state of development of the universe, of the living world, and of the human species obliges me, in all strictness, to questioning, to incompleteness or to relativity. It is not, therefore, a question of uttering a truth valid once and for all but of trying to make a gesture, faithful to the reality of yesterday and to that of today, that indicates a path toward more continuity, less tearing apart, more interiority, concentration, harmony—in me, between me and the living universe, between me and the other(s), if that is or becomes possible, as I hope it is, given respect for the living universe and its temporality.

I return then to Schopenhauer in order to ask some questions starting from his texts, which I have not yet read exhaustively. According to him, I have therefore read nothing. And I understand this irritation of the author who takes care over his journey and to whom only a part is returned. But Schopenhauer believes that there is not great progress in our development. He also teaches that the human species will be condensed, without differentiation or evolution, in him as in each human being. Certain chapters of his writings reveal therefore the whole of his work and even the whole of the truth of the man that he is, even of the humanity that he claims to recapitulate in himself.

I will not linger over his *Essay on Women*, except to underline that this text is not at all the inverse of his work as Didier Raymond, who wrote the preface to the French edition, claims it to be. It finds a totally coherent place there. I am going to try to make that clear.

I am only astonished that, while so many women have intelligent things to say and so many men are still unknown, a publisher cared to print such a little book, and at such a price. That confirms what Schopenhauer reveals to us, among other truths: philosophy is a matter of death. A philosopher living and thinking life is a priori suspect in our philosophical culture. Thus begins the chapter "On Death and Its Relation to the Indestructibility of Our Inner Nature" (2:463) in *The World as Will and Representation*: "Death is the real inspiring genius or Musagetes of philosophy, and for this reason Socrates defined philosophy as *thanatou mélétè* (preparation for death; Plato, *Phaedo*, 81a). Indeed, without death there would hardly have been any philosophizing. It will therefore be quite in order for a special consideration of this subject to have its place here at the beginning of the last, most serious, and most important of our books."[1]

I will begin from this chapter as well as those entitled "The Metaphysics of Sexual Love," "On the Vanity and Suffering of

Life," "The Hereditary Nature of Qualities," "On the Possibility of Knowing the Thing-in-Itself," "On the Primacy of the Will in Self-Consciousness."

I will not make precise references to them. I have constructed my analysis more particularly in relation to these chapters. Which does not exclude a reading of the texts *On Vision and Colors* and *On the Will in Nature*, a reading that has not contradicted until now the interpretation of Schopenhauer that I am going to sketch in order to interrogate it.

SCHOPENHAUER'S PHILOSOPHICAL INTENTION

Schopenhauer's metaphysics can be defined, according to me, as *biological materialism*. The will of which he speaks does not correspond to a will of the becoming of the spirit nor even of the flesh, that is, to an individuation. It is a blind pathos of the reproduction of the species. For Schopenhauer what we designate generally as a duty to reproduce, to give birth, is linked to the most obscure and elementary passion of man. Of man, in effect. Because the will is, according to him, masculine, and intelligence is feminine. The reproduction of the species is therefore a concern of man. But this passion or this *dynamis* corresponds to the substance of metaphysics and of transcendence.

Contrary to what we have generally been taught, metaphysics, according to Schopenhauer, is not situated in an ascending economy of forms, of norms, of ideas more and more transcendent to the sensible and to matter. No. Metaphysics resides in the dynamism of reproductive chromosomes that tear man away from his individual being. I am—Schopenhauer asserts—projected outside of myself by my will to reproduce the species. Love between lovers represents nothing but an irresistible reproductive attraction. Their sorrows and groanings—Schopenhauer speaks little of their joys . . . —are only those of the species and nothing can oppose them. As individuals, the lovers do not exist, and both men and women are treated here in the same way. Neither the one nor the other exist and they are differentiated only by the hierarchy of natural functions. There too, contrary to what could be expected, the will prevails over intelligence. Would I dare to say that the old brain prevails over the new? That is neither totally correct nor totally exact. But the allusion will make it clear, if need be, that once again Schopenhauer confounds our habitual ways of thinking. We have been taught that women were passionate and men intelligent, capable of sublimating their passions. For Schopenhauer it is nothing like this. But if you think, as women, that you will find here some kind of valorization, you are wrong: intelligence is only a passive emanation of the will. The least flick of the will makes it change opinion. No intelligence—not even that of men, unless they are beings of great genius—can resist the will.

Thus Schopenhauer's metaphysics does without representable formal ideals, without overtly confessed divine transcendence; the transcendence of the other is not claimed there either. The transcendence of metaphysics resides in the genius of the species that merges with the masculine will to reproduce.

Before laughing too quickly, it would be fitting to make sure that what Schopenhauer expresses is not hidden in the majority of philosophies called Western, more exactly in philosophical discourse starting from a certain epoch of domination of culture by patriarchy. In other words, does not Schopenhauer go to the end of things by bringing to light that which most veil with a maya, an art of illusion, that is more or less clever and blinding? Does not Schopenhauer attest altogether bluntly what others do without saying or knowing it: philosophy corresponds to an absolute patriarchalism and it is a matter of death?

Does not what is described as pessimism in Schopenhauer's work correspond, at least in part, to the revelation of an elementary truth that has founded metaphysics for ages, at least in our cultures? Man essentially wants to reproduce, nothing can stop him from doing this, not even the intelligence of women, and this will, when it does not produce natural children, gives birth to imaginary children. Philosophy and religion are two of them. This necessity of reproduction would correspond to the genius of the species of which men are the guardians.

Thus man is the slave of a genius, of the genius that obliges him to transcend himself in and by reproduction. Schopenhauer often confines his discussion to natural reproduction. It seems to me that the reproduction that is called spiritual grows from the same will as long as it is not interpreted in the light of such revelations. Schopenhauer says it. Nietzsche asserts it very explicitly: his works are his children.

So all of metaphysics is neatly overturned by Schopenhauer or, more exactly, pursued all the way to its root and beyond. Its dynamis is the work of the will inscribed in the masculine seed. Truth would not be as transcendent as it is attested, discreetly but in an authoritarian way, or its transcendence is the work of maya that blinds the philosophers themselves. Unveiled, truth is spermatic. *Logos spermatikos*, if one prefers to invoke it or evoke it in another language and in a field not directly philosophical in order to maintain a little of its mystery.

Schopenhauer's questioning, at first glance naive, is fundamental. And every truth would have significance setting out again from this biological revelation. How to interpret this position of the philosophical unveiled by Schopenhauer? How to interpret the work of Schopenhauer himself? How to give his work a meaning or a future other than those that he proposes? All of which could be restated another way: how to reconstruct what he deconstructs?

THE PERSPECTIVE OF THE GENUS

Two places can serve as fulcrums or as sites for putting Schopenhauer's philosophy into perspective. They are not foreign to one another:

1. The question, to some extent natural, of the difference of the sexes that Schopenhauer treats in a biologically inexact manner. Let us say, for example, that he confuses genus and species.

2. The Hindu tradition to which Schopenhauer appeals in order to hold his discourse and which, unlike his own truths and will, never distances itself from the body or from nature as micro- and macrocosm, which it is a matter of cultivating with the aim of winning the happiness of immortality or of eternity while discharging one's human task.

According to me these two sites—the tradition of India and the question of the cultural status of sexual difference—are linked, inasmuch as "Hinduism, such as it appears since the end of the Middle Ages, represents the synthesis, but with a marked predominance of aboriginal factors,"[2] of Indo-European and pre-Aryan aboriginal Asiatic cultures. The cul-

tures of Hinduism would have resisted the influence of patriarchy and its economy: pastoral, nomadic, celestial, atmos-
pheric, through a defense of places, in particular the earth and
its plants and foods, through the respect for traditions of the
mother and of woman, more faithful to life in its concrete
aspects, to religion in its perceptible and mystical dimension.
The contribution of patriarchalized Indo-Europeans consist-
ing among other things in ritualism and philosophical and
religious speculations.

Thanks to this presence of feminine traditions, India has
retained traces of pre-patriarchal cultures. It has also devel-
oped certain cultural dimensions that we have nearly forgotten. In India men and women are gods together, and together
they create the world, including its cosmic dimension. The
divine couples, whether it is Vishnu or Shiva, along with their
lovers, are microcosms in constant economic relations with
the macrocosm; the same goes for Tantrism. These couples are
generally represented without children. They are lovers, and
lovers of the universe.

We are far here from Schopenhauer's genius of the species.
We are close to a possible philosophy, wisdom, or religion of
sexual difference of which India is perhaps one of the places
of emergence or of subsistence.

But of which India does Schopenhauer speak? Which India
is evoked in Western philosophy, when it is evoked? The

greater part of the Hindu tradition remains unknown to it except in the case of some practitioners of the Vedas, of yoga, of mantras, of the texts or the art of India. But these people most often know the Western philosophical tradition poorly and do not secure the possible passages between the two traditions, or at least they fail or are reluctant to do it. The only chance for a correct interpretation of Hindu thought is found nevertheless with these men, or women, because this Indian culture does not separate theory and practice, notably in love. And we risk interpreting it very badly if we do not approach it with an appropriate practice. It seems that this misunderstanding exists, for example in the work of Schopenhauer. He has retained certain elements of the Indian tradition, but has he not perverted these in taking them out of their framework, this word being understood with a rigor to which we are little accustomed? I would like to give some examples of this concerning 1. temporality in the strict sense, 2. the practice of philosophy, 3. the interpretation of suffering and the joy of living, 4. the intention concerning the will to live, 5. the question of individuation, 6. the question of the status of knowledge.

ARTHUR SCHOPENHAUER'S EGOLOGICAL CONFUSIONS

1. Time, temporality, in India could not belong to the genius of the human species alone. This egological, egocentric, pas-

sion is unknown to the diverse traditions of India. Man is
never at the center there, but he also is not "less than," "not as
good as" some animal for example, as he would be according
to Schopenhauer's statements. Man *is*, and, inasmuch as he is,
he must devote himself to being at the service of macro- or
microcosmic temporality. The Vedas, the Upanishads, and
yoga have for their principal function to assure the articulation between the instant and immortality or eternity. Sometimes it is above all a matter of constituting or creating a
macrocosmic unity through rites relative to the days, to the
seasons, to the years, rites practiced among others by the
Brahmins; sometimes the accent is put on the realization of a
unity or individual immortality, even an eternity, through the
control of breathing, thanks in particular to yoga but also to
the Upanishads.[3] Nothing is more foreign to the traditions of
India than the metaphysical pathos of reproduction. This
could only be a Western translation of the respect for life supposing it evoked happiness. But that does not amount to the
same thing. Thus the Vedic gods, the Brahmins, and the yogis
care about the maintenance of the life of the universe and
that of their body as cosmic nature. They care about them at
each moment. Their task is to articulate a continuity between
the present and immortality or eternity. The question that I
would pose on this subject is, Why is the present time perceived as discontinuous? Or, starting from what or when is it

thus perceived? By whom? I am going to return to this. I wanted to emphasize that, unlike the traditions of India, the time of life, according to Schopenhauer, is no more than an abstract survival of the species whose cause is situated before my birth or after my death. The present, unless it be an a priori framework, is for Schopenhauer no more than an unfortunate and passively suffered temporality between these two moments that escape my will but determine it. No present or presence for Schopenhauer. The gods of India, the Brahmins, the yogis are, on the contrary, in the present, or they start from it and look for the means to repair, to reestablish, a torn up cosmic time through the constitution of immortality or of eternity for the universe and for oneself.

2. I can try to make this understood speculatively. In order to comprehend it or, rather, to realize it effectively, it is fitting *to do, to act*. That does not mean recourse to some more or less occult or accessible cult or initiation. Certainly, it is necessary to learn the practice from one who knows it. The same goes for philosophy or grammar in our civilization. What I wanted to signal is that the present, temporality, the relation between the instant and immortality or eternity is constituted by *acts*, and not only by words, logical and grammatical conventions, already coded meaning, a prioris, etc. These acts, realized by certain Brahmins or yogis, for example, are not ritualized in the way we have a tendency to understand it. That is, they are

not simply repetitive. They obtain the sought after efficacy—namely, the passage between present, past, and future—only if they are well done, well articulated, and well articulating. They vary therefore from one day to another, because the present time changes from one day to the next. What we could interpret as ritualism or boring asceticism signifies, for these practitioners, the accomplishment of acts, of gestures, appropriate for linking the body to the universe, the instant to duration, etc. They aim at a plenitude, at obtaining the status of immortals by surmounting the discontinuity of time; they are a contribution to the happiness of the self and of the world through the exercise of daily practices. Why daily? Because the day is the unit of measure. The season is another unit, the year yet another one.

We are unaccustomed to hearing this discourse concerning India because our tradition, since the golden age of the Greeks in particular, has begun to break the continuity between micro- and macrocosm. Philosophy, religion (apart from the liturgy celebrating the times of the year?), language, progress have become constructions of a socio-logical subject cut off from its cosmo-logical, bio-logical rootedness. In other words, science, knowledge are here generally relative to a social status of the individual and not to the articulation between micro- and macrocosm, body and universe, physical and spiritual temporality, present and eternity, etc. What we call metaphysics corresponds, in its negative side, to an ill-considered sacrifice of the body and of the universe to a coded and codeable knowledge outside a *present* act, to a truth that is valid in all times and all places.

This sacrifice is accompanied by the decline of the divine character of sexual difference, by the destruction of feminine religious traditions and of cultural, worshipful relations between mothers and daughters and between women. This is to the benefit of masculine genealogies alone.

The positive aspect that is invoked is the establishment of a democracy. I think that it would be necessary to reflect very rigorously on the destructive means employed for the establishment of this democracy, on the fact that it signifies the substitution of a public power practiced between men alone for a social order in which all human beings participate in the management of the civil and religious order.

A democracy in which only men exercise power and elect the officials of the city is, from the beginning, undemocratic. We have not finished observing its destructive fallout and impasses, including in the dissociation between the spoken, speakable discourses and the actions undertaken. Including in the gaps between coded truth and the demands of our time as well.

3. In India, at least according to tradition, the word remains gesture, in particular a phonatory one, and acts or movements

cannot be separated from it. We have forgotten this because of patriarchal censorships and repressions carried out upon the relation of truth to the corporeal, to the sexual, to the macrocosm. Even the Buddha and Buddhism are sometimes used to further this forgetting and misunderstanding of the tradition of India, including in its association with a nihilistic pessimism. It is true that the Buddha goes away from what is not going well in the present with a view to liberation, to detachment. But that does not imply a negative judgment on the present nor on life, quite the contrary. Renunciation, for the Buddha, represents the way of access to continuity and to harmony. To practice renunciation does not signify, for him, sacrificing oneself for a hypothetical immortality or eternity but bringing them about here and now. Such work cannot be carried out in a purely speculative manner, which is another Western error in the interpretation of the Buddha's teaching. He never separated himself from the economy of the living universe, notably the vegetal. If he renounces—at least according to our perspective—it is because the objects of desire, the objective correlates of my subjective desires, oppose harmony with the universal breath. They tear me to pieces. The quest of the Buddha seems to me to correspond to the search for a continuous communion with the respiration of the macrocosm. In order to attain such fluidity, the Buddha renounces the punctuality, the discontinuity, of objects and, moreover, of discourses. He tries to become pure subject but on a model forgotten by us: pure subject means here breathing in tune with the breathing of the entire living universe. If there is suffering in living, it is that this universal and continuous communication or communion is difficult to carry out. It is not a question, for all that, of wishing for death, because if death happens before this education of the breath, of the subject as breath, it means going back where all would start over again, and worse . . .

But the Buddha cannot be understood without the Vedic gods, the Brahmins, the Upanishads, yoga, etc. We make of him an export product abstracted from his practice, from his truth, if we thoughtlessly take him out of the places and the times of his coming. We also misinterpret him if we reduce him to discourse—including by using him to critique Western discursivity—while forgetting his gestures. The Buddha makes himself gestures. He even gives up speaking, undoubtedly because speaking harmonizes with breathing with difficulty—except in song and poetry?—and brings discontinuity to it. Moreover, speaking generally supposes an object of speech. Now the Buddha renounces every object, the object always being partial, nonabsolute, a cause of conflicts, sorrows.

4. But to renounce objects, once more, does not mean renouncing life. The time of life, in most of the traditions of

India (which correspond to the evolution of a single thought where what is at stake is precisely the question of time), corresponds to the time of cultivating my life in harmony with that of the universe. Philosophies and/or religions present themselves in India as *practices* the intention of which is to live the happiest life possible thanks to the renunciation of that which hinders living, particularly in harmony with the living universe, its past, its present, and its future. These practices aim, among other things or principally, at realizing the immortality or the eternity of the self and of the world here and now. The meaning of the philosophical and religious practices of the Indian tradition is misunderstood most of the time, notably as concerns the time of life and its economy seeking to attain the absolute happiness of immortality or eternity here below. Detachment has for its goal the end of misfortune, of illusion tied to the *partial* character of the truth. These philosophical and religious practices are not without intention, as is often presented to us, or as we risk imagining it; they are, on the contrary, evaluated according to their efficacy. But their intention should be understood in a different sense than the one we generally give to this word. Intention does not aim at an exterior object or project with the objective of an appropriation, of a consumption, or of a possession. Intention has as its objective the constitution of an accomplished interiority that remains tied to and in con-

stant communion with the whole of the world. If you are
having trouble grasping what is at issue, perhaps the contemplation of certain representations of the Buddha in medita-
tion will be able to convey to you something of the nature of
his intention.

5. These few elements of the Indian tradition seem rather
different from the use that Schopenhauer makes of them. Yet
I chose them in response to what he cites of this culture. I
have not spoken of Vishnu, of Krishna, of Shiva and of their
loves, for example. Now these philosophico-religious representations are not less important than the others, including in
popular practices but also in those of certain Brahmins and
yogis of India today. They are closer to feminine aboriginal
cultures, thus more foreign still to the Western philosopher
than the Buddha is. But already certain misunderstandings
appear evident in what Schopenhauer recovers from the
Hindu tradition:

—There can be no question, in this culture, of sacrificing
the individual for the species. Every living being—human,
animal, plant, or element of the universe—is considered here
with very great respect. Moreover, the Hindus do not at all
worship reproduction. The loving couple that they form generally reproduces two children out of consideration for the
order of the living. They are two and they engender two children. This is their contribution to the time of the world: mor-

tal and immortal. Finally, the Hindus worship individuation as body, as self, but not as ego. Now is not Schopenhauer's genius of the species in fact egological?

—The species, according to the traditions of India, cannot be reduced to one genus, nor the genius of the human species to the masculine gender. The gods, including the god of gods, Vishnu, create the universe with their lovers. It is their loves that give birth to the micro- and macrocosm, it is their amorous misfortunes that destroy them. The two are evoked together, embracing, and in relation with the elements of the universe. These are represented as exterior but linked to a part of the body: thus Vishnu often has a foot in the water and Shiva often has fire in his hand.

To be sure, there are in India tensions between feminine aboriginal cultures and patriarchal Aryan cultures. It is significant that Western philosophy recovers only the most Aryan elements of the Indian tradition. Instead of transforming this error into conflicts between men, it would seem more useful to understand that it is always a question of a choice of men to the detriment of pre-patriarchal cultures still living in India. If we confine ourselves to theoretical and political quarrels between men, nothing allows us to get out of these conflicts, as murderous as they are. That mediating third is lacking, the real existence of which the pre-patriarchal cultures of India still manifest today.

6. Thus Brahma, invoked by certain Western intellectuals as the place of the neuter par excellence, can be identified only by his place in relation to the other divine couples, in particular in corporeal geography. Brahma is situated at the summit. He is the last born of the divine genealogy, perhaps a child of Shiva and Uma Parvati. But:

—Brahma is often represented as a child (as is the case with Krishna and Jesus). The gods of the head, which have been represented to us as the excellence of masculine intelligence and the place of its authority over the feminine body, are represented more and more as boys with the advance of patriarchalized History, but they are children or adolescents. The gods of the word would seem not yet to have acquired their completed forms, especially human and especially sexual. They are still children, ill-defined sexually (Krishna has a very feminine aspect and Jesus is sometimes defined as the most feminine of all men).

—Brahma is also represented as a hybrid of the human species and other kingdoms. So he is sometimes evoked as a flower, born of the lotus. Concerning this, it would be worthwhile to remind Schopenhauer of the mode of plant reproduction. It is involuntary, dependent upon other species or other kingdoms: butterflies, insects, or winds, for example.

—Brahma is accompanied by a bird, like most of the practitioners of the Indian tradition (between the Father and the Son, between Mary and Jesus as well, the Spirit is thus represented).

—Brahma fears the natural elements, particularly the wind. When the god of winds, Vac, menaces him or threatens, he takes refuge in a blade of grass; he takes root again. He no longer argues. He gives up his summits. He returns to the earth (the wind is another attribute of the spirit).

—Brahma asks questions. His genius is not to know everything but to be capable of one more question. Far from being certain, Brahma always remains in a questioning state. Under no circumstances does Brahma represent a neuter universal who can be extrapolated from his context, abstracted from the universe—an abstraction that is universalizable because it is neuter. Brahma exists only through the capacity to pose a question beyond what already exists, for thus he assures becoming, especially between air and ether. The genius of Brahma is the art of posing questions and not that of elaborating a closed system. In this, Brahma is faithful to the temporality of natural growth, from which the greatest part of Indian practices cannot stray. To be sure, Brahma is supposed to assure a joining between earth and sky, but that mediation remains incarnated. It is child, flower, blade of grass, element of the universe. It is also linked to the animal world by the bird. It is subjected to the macrocosmic kingdom, especially to the will for breathing. Moreover, this mediation is always becoming, always in the form of a question. Mediation for Brahma would not be exercised once and for all. Will and intelligence are in perpetual growth and interaction. Brahma wants to assure the passage from air to ether. He can only do it through the mediation of questions. If his will exceeds his intelligence, Vac gets angry. Brahma must again become a blade of grass, a plant, in order to save his life, life itself, intelligence.

THE GENIUS OF THE SPECIES AND
THE HINDU TRADITION

The genius of the species, according to Schopenhauer, has a relation to the traditions of India in so much as it does not forget the physiological in favor of a discursive truth said to be valid for men, women, and everything. But he only goes back to one part of this biological or physiological, which distorts its truth.

The genius of the species is pre-Hindu—if that can be said—inasmuch as it is pessimistic as concerns human individuation. That is marked by two points above all:

—Human development, according to Schopenhauer, is not necessarily better than animal development. Respecting all the incarnations of life, the Indian does not, for all that, place all these incarnations on the same plane because *we must become gods as men and women.* For this development, there are stages, a temporality, corresponding notably to the progressive spiritualization of different parts of the body. This spiritualization can be realized alone or in couples with a more experienced practitioner. There is always a part of the development that remains solitary, tied to individuation.

—There is no spiritualization of the body in Schopenhauer. This lack goes hand in hand, it seems to me, with his impression that suffering is inevitable, with his contempt for the feminine gender, with his relationship to death, with his exasperated passions (manifest in his correspondence with Goethe, for example). To be sure, Schopenhauer must have been an unbeliever. But he looks to establish a transcendence and he does not find any other than that of the human species as species. He searches, as is done in India, for a transcendence that is in part immanent. To do this he is required to sacrifice individuation and all forms of spiritual development. It seems to me that Schopenhauer could have learned from the traditions of India that the divine is not situated in an inaccessible transcendence. It is what I become, what I create. I become and I create (the) god(s) between immanence and transcendence. The rupture between immanence and transcendence is due, it seems to me, to 1. the constitution of the divine as logos having all power over the natural universe, although it is produced by only one part of this universe, at a moment of its history, 2. the release of each man and each woman from concern for realizing each day the passage from the microcosm to the macrocosm, from the mortal to the immortal, from tearing apart to unity, 3. the substitution of the creation of a totality potentially completed by a God referred to as belonging to the masculine gender for the continuous generation of the world in its material and spiritual dimension.

The genius of the species would still be pre-Hindu insofar as it fails to recognize that the fulfillment of the human species, its nonregression to animality, can only come about through the deification of the two human genders: men and women (and not only as mother and son) and their carnal as well as spiritual love.

It seems that Schopenhauer doubts the immortality of the human species. Does not this uncertainty, which is transformed into metaphysical will, result from the will to reproduce (oneself) as masculine pathos, functioning outside of all love and recognition of a feminine gender capable of transcendence?

STRATIFICATIONS NECESSARY FOR THE TIME OF LIFE

This transcendence of the feminine as gender is related to the time of the vegetable kingdom, plants and flowers, to the animal kingdom by the bird, to the universal economy by earth, water, wind. If Aristotle leaves woman at best to the vegetal world, and at worst to chaos and the void, this is not an accident. But, even this relation of the most speculative to the most vegetal, of the most vegetal to the most speculative, of which Brahma still testifies and which attests—in Greek terms—that *hyle*, *dynamis*, and *morphe* cannot be separated, this relation has become foreign to us. The death in which the philosopher is interested is without doubt the symptom of this interruption of the growth and blossoming of matter of which the feminine, in particular, is victim because of the lack of subjectivation of her nature.

In Western philosophy the thought of the world as a living world no longer exists. Nor does the thought of sexual difference. Logos is supposed to express cosmos and to give an account for all being, including the gods. That has rendered the truth a priori timeless and fixed. The truth must be, once and for all, immortal or eternal: immortal for ideas and gods, eternal for God.

Diverse strata necessary for the constitution of time are therefore abolished. Thus:

1. The time of life is always partly *cyclical*, like the time of the seasons and of the vegetal or vegetative universe. Now philosophy splits up into philosophy of the fluent, of the timeless, or of the cyclical without perceiving that it is a mat-

ter of choices that are not very conscious with respect to the time of life.

In the same way, the cyclical character of feminine sexuality is little appreciated by the upholders of truth, like that of the cycles of the moon and even of the earth. And the models relative to masculine sexuality characterize its energy as reversible with return to homeostasis, that is to say as immutable.

2. The time of life is partly *growth*. The vegetal remains tied to the cyclical and to growth. This development of life has been fixed in definitive forms. It reappears in the form of comparisons, scales of values, etc.

3. The time of life is *irreversible*. Which is also in part denied by Western philosophies.

4. The time of life has become in the West an effect of social organizations and conventions, of socio-logical projections upon living reality:

a) a submission to patriarchal genealogical order, substituting itself for natural engendering, either cosmic or maternal;

b) a social and political organization between humans— which has meant, in fact, between men—founded upon sacrificial rites and not upon cosmological rhythms;

c) a substitution of the reproduction of the human species for the becoming of the living world as a whole;

d) an institution of History as human time that is cumulative but not necessarily progressive, which leads to disorder, entropy, chaos.

The time of life has become a socio-logical temporality founded on a second (or double) nature of man that has caused him to lose his relation to the living world. Women are supposed to carry out the task of guarding this relation while men attend to the work of a universal without a natural, if not arbitrary, substratum, constructed by one part of humanity. What assures this torn and artificial temporality are logical structures founded in particular upon the principles of identity and resemblance, upon the principle of noncontradiction, that is to say upon the definition of a second nature the poles of which are no longer day and night, the seasons, the ages of life, but, at best, the oscillating from the true to the false, from a clear to an obscure that are called spiritual, from a speculative day to its night.

Nothing of this pendulum of the universe that we are, particularly through our hearing, remains in these lacerations and oscillations. Buddha knew this—and maybe all the Boddhisattvas. He had to learn it by meditating under the tree, by spiritualizing his senses, by becoming familiar with the price of compassion.

Because what is at stake in the Indian traditions—but not only in these—aside from the passage from the present to immortality or to eternity, is the correlative question of the heaviness or lightness of bodies. This question calls for much wisdom and love in order to begin to be perceived. It demands thinking and putting into practice two poles of attraction:

—that which ties me to cosmological attractions, notably to earthly heaviness but also to solar or lunar attraction;

—that which ties me to others, in particular to the other of sexual difference.

We still know almost nothing of this appeal or attraction, an important element of wisdom and of divinity.

Familiarity with the tradition of India can put us on or put us back on the way, or, at least, challenge us.

Eastern Teachings

To explain what Western culture has given me—and not given me—and what the practice of yoga and its tradition have given me—and not given me—is not a simple task to carry out. In the development of a life it is not always easy, in effect, to distinguish what comes from one source and what comes from another. However, I am going to try to formulate—at the request of François Lorin to whom I owe much knowledge acquired thanks to yoga—some contributions and deficiencies of this tradition that seem to me rather clearly identifiable at this time, at the level of experiences and of knowledge that are mine.

What Yoga Has Taught (or Reminded) Me

What I have learned from yoga—beyond or on this side of my Western culture—are things about existence that are both very simple and very subtle.

TO BREATHE AND TO SPEAK

First, I learned to breathe. Breathing, according to me, corresponds to taking charge of one's own life. Only the mother, during pregnancy, breathes in place of the child. After birth, whoever does not breathe, does not respect his or her own life and takes air from the other, from others. Breathing is thus a duty toward my life, that of others, and that of the entire living world. Because the majority of people in our age do not treat with care the time of breathing, it is necessary—in any case, it is necessary for me, but I think that this necessity is general—to go for walks or to remain a moment each day in the vegetal world in order to continue to breathe and to live outside of the surrounding social exploitation.

yes

It is also necessary to understand the relations between respiration and other acts, in particular the act of speaking. Breathing and speaking use breath in an almost inverse manner, in any case for the majority of people. From this point of view it is interesting to note that people who do not breathe, or who breathe poorly, cannot stop speaking. It is their way of breathing, and notably of exhaling in order to draw another breath. Frequently, they also paralyze the breathing of whoever takes corporeal and spiritual care of his or her breath, of the breath of others. To remain silently attentive to the breath comes down to respecting that which, or who, exists and maintaining for oneself the possibility to be born and to create.

On this subject it is important to meditate on the fact that a spirituality or a religion centered on speech, without insistence on breathing and the silence that makes it possible, risks supporting a nonrespect for life. In such traditions the act of using breath to define more or less definitive words, of using nature and living bodies to develop a social worship becomes destructive because of a lack of recognition and regeneration of this contribution of life. Such spiritual and religious practices or theories quickly become authoritarian through the immobilization of breathing. They become dogmatic by forgetting the gift that comes from the living world—in particular the vegetal world—and from human bodies—in particular female bodies. Unfortunately most patriarchal philosophical and religious traditions act in this way: they have substituted words for life without carrying out the necessary links between the two. Now it is these links that would allow reciprocally conserving, regenerating, and enriching life and speech.

There is an example of this that people of the Christian tradition know well. The Annunciation, which precedes the
birth of Jesus, can be interpreted in at least two different
ways: as the substitution of the word of the celestial Father
for corporeal relations, notably of breathing, between two
lovers or as the fact that, in order to engender a spiritual
child—a possible savior of the world—the conception of
this savior must be preceded by an announcement through
speech and by a response from Mary. It is not a question then
of miraculous birth by a woman who is supposed to have
kept her hymen, but of an engendering preceded by an
exchange of breath and of words between the future lovers
and parents. The angel, the bird, the ray of the sun, and speech
represent the mediations between the body of Mary and that
of the Lord. All these mediations indicate relations between
the body and speech without substituting the one for the
other, as a certain type of teaching would like to make us
"believe." They signify that a spiritual engendering cannot
take place without the coming into play of breathing and the
controlled expression of this breathing between the lovers.
The current account of the "angelic greeting" would appear,
from this point of view, partially erroneous in the sense that
the words do not respect the question of the messenger to
Mary: "Do you want to be the mother of the/a savior?"
Without this question the Annunciation risks evoking the

imposition of a patriarchal order on a virgin adolescent bound to another man: "Mary, the Lord informs you that you will be the mother of his child." There are no longer, in this case, two persons: Mary becomes the simple vehicle at the service of giving birth to the son of a God-the-Father. But, if there are no longer two persons, there is no longer respect for the breath between them, nor respect for Mary's spiritual virginity. The first interpretation, close to feminine aboriginal traditions (including by virtue of the necessarily oral character of the announcement), seems to me more capable of translating a spiritual message, which would then be forgotten and subjected to the authoritarian power of a word that supposedly has to supplant the body and not make it divine as such.

Unfortunately, patriarchal traditions have progressively replaced life with speech without assuring between them relations capable of allowing each to enrich the other. The uncontrolled proliferation of techniques, unhealthy urbanization, the pollution of the universe, submission to money, wars, including ideological ones, have followed from this. As well as the progressive sclerosis of the mental and the physical.

In the passage from traditions that respect the breath to those that submit (themselves) to speech without concern for the breath, the mode of speaking has evolved from poetic

saying, from the hymn of song, from the prayer of praise to
use already written discourses or texts, often in the imperative,
addressing the individual in his relation to society more than
to the cosmos, an individual whose paradigm is the adult man
subject to the authority of the often absent gods of his gender. The most spiritual becoming proposed then to woman is
that she also can be a man . . . In our egalitarian times, one can
note the return, including on the part of certain feminists, to
religious texts that announce nothing better to women than
to be equal to men! I would compare, on this occasion, the
forgetting of feminine aboriginal traditions, particularly of
India, with the submission of women to patriarchal power in
the horizon of which the ideal, for them, would be to
become men.

In this patriarchal horizon the very use of speech and the
circulation of breath have changed. Speech finds itself subjected to ritual, to repetition, to speculation. It has been
uprooted from its present engendering, in relation with the
rest of the energy of the body and of the world that surrounds it. The writing of a poem, the singing of praise—pos-
sibly addressed to nature, to the lover, to a divinity that we
use incarnate or could incarnate—use respiration in a way other
than obedience to an already written word or text, express-
ing orders or laws, more than praises or graces. In the first case
we remain closer to the divinities that guard life and cultivate

it. We are these gods or goddesses who protect, engender, or deploy life, divinities always tied to nature and not simply produced or chosen by a people or a society.

In my case, the consciousness of being a woman, the desire to remain a woman and to spiritually become a woman found in the practice of yoga and the reading of certain ancient texts of this tradition an aid for interpreting my more patriarchal tradition and for reviving a repressed culture that better suits me. Such a culture is lacking today for the spiritualization of a society of men and of women and, especially, for the spiritualization of love between them: at the level of the couple or of society, a love remaining in harmony with the natural living universe that serves us as a place of existence and of regeneration.

TO RESPECT AND TO CULTIVATE SENSIBLE PERCEPTIONS

In patriarchal traditions individual and collective life both wants to and believes it is able to organize itself outside of the surroundings of the natural world. The body—also called microcosm—is then cut off from the universe—which is called macrocosm. It is submitted to sociological rules, to rhythms foreign to its sensibility, to its living perceptions: day and night, seasons, vegetal growth . . . This means that acts of participation in light, sounds or music, odors, touch, or even in natural tastes are no longer cultivated as human qualities. The body is no longer educated to develop its perceptions spiritually, but to detach itself from the sensible for a more abstract, more speculative, more sociological culture.

Yoga taught me to return to the cultivation of sensible perception. In fact, I have always loved it. Since my childhood, nature has helped me and has taught me how to live. But yoga brought me back to this taste with texts that lead me from the innocence of sensations to a spiritual elaboration that permits their development, and sometimes their communication or sharing.

To be sure, Western culture has produced an art that doubles, in some fashion, the contributions of nature: painting, music, the art of cooking, etc. But it seems that art cannot be substituted for the experience of natural perceptions. It can help in enduring the absence of this contribution without claiming to replace it. For example, at night, when the birds sleep, listening to music is good. But music does not correspond to the living present of the singing of birds. It is perhaps more in one sense, but less in another. It is most often already repetition, unless it is an improvisation, in particular vocal, unique. That is rare. And, moreover, it is possible that humans have lost the capacity that birds have of singing in harmony with the state of the universe, of celebrating nature such as it is in the moment.

Another aspect: Western mysticism has cultivated perceptions that are secondary. It speaks of a touch, of a taste of the "spirit," for example. But these spiritual discoveries, often acquired at the expense of great suffering, do not seem to me to be able to substitute themselves for the cultivation of sensible perceptions. Learning to listen to beautiful sounds, to contemplate beautiful colors, to taste good products of the earth aids spiritual development. I prefer this nonsacrificial path to another. And we do not have enough of an existence to educate our sensible faculties. Why repress them for a hypothetical beyond? That appears to me today to be not very holy or very wise. And the transformation of my body into a spiritual body seems a lot more worthwhile than access to a science, including that of God, that scorns the body and leads it onto paths of useless and sterile suffering.

In order to cultivate the body, it is necessary to remain close to cosmic rhythms. The liturgy and Christian monastic orders have been aware of this. Too often, this dimension is unfortunately forgotten. So, yet again, why speak of spiritual "night," of spiritual "drought," of spiritual "winter" while neglecting the impact upon us of the real "night," of the real "drought," of the real "winter"? All this metaphorical language leads to a lot of mortifying wanderings.

TO LEARN AND TO TEACH

Something else that yoga taught me or clarified for me is the necessity of a living link between the teacher and the student. The Western tradition has often wanted to dissociate the one from the other. Education in the West is then assimilated to apprenticeship or to the reading of texts, the dead authors of which are often more appreciated than living ones. It is subjected to writing with a minimal part of transmission being truly oral. It makes of the teacher an aseptic and supposedly neuter vehicle of the culture that he/she transmits.

According to me, to learn, in the best of cases, is to learn from someone's experience. To teach is to transmit an experience. What is taught is guaranteed by the life of the one who teaches, and by that of his or her own masters. In this way a concrete and spiritual knowledge is elaborated, a knowledge useful for a cultivation of life, for which the life of the teacher himself remains the support of truth, of ethics, and even of aesthetics. This practice of teaching constitutes a genealogy that is at the same time natural and cultural. In certain families knowledge is handed down from father to son, from mother to daughter, from father to daughter, from mother to son. In other cultural lineages the transmission occurs outside the natural family, from master to disciple. But, remaining linked to experience, it engenders a sort of milieu that is at once natural, sensible, and spiritual where knowledge of the past circulates and where that of the present and the future is elaborated. Indeed, a culture tied to experience cannot be reduced to the repetition of an already written corpus. Such a culture evolves, be it only according to the evolution of the universe, but also in the way of thinking the link between cosmic history and the history of living beings, particularly human beings, of this world.

For the transmission of culture to be correct, it is necessary to notice the differences between what women's experience can teach us and what men's experience can teach us, without privileging the teaching coming from one sex or from one gender. In fact, it is not true that knowledge is indifferent to sex or gender. The most daily experience teaches us this as does the knowledge of tradition, including that of yoga. The corporeal and spiritual experience of a woman is singular, and what she can teach of it to her daughter and to her son is not the same. To efface this contribution of the transmission of culture is to falsify its truth and value. It is also to contribute to teaching's becoming more and more ritual, speculative, magical, tied to the worship of the father and to

exclusively celestial divinities, constructed by the spirit of
men as incorporeal, and even timeless, guarantees of texts and
laws organizing their societies. It is then no longer a matter of
living human divinities, of gods and goddesses among us such
as exist in feminine aboriginal traditions and what remains of
them, but of absolutes recapitulating an epoch of History in
order to gather together, to organize, to rationalize its multiple dimensions. A teaching linked to earthly life, to the sensible, to the concrete, and concerned with cultivating their
fecundity as well as their spiritual, divine, mystical qualities is
a mode of transmission more faithful to the oldest traditions,
particularly those of yoga. These traditions are feminine,
which does not mean maternal. The accent put solely on the
maternity of women is rather a masculine perspective in the
evolution of the tradition.

TO LIVE SPIRITUALLY THE BODY AND THE FLESH

This different mode of approaching life, others, teaching—
that I have learned or relearned from yoga—supposes and
accompanies a singular experience of the body. It has often
been said to me that I should have conquered my body, that
I should have subjected it to spirit. The development of spirit
was presented to me in the form of philosophical or religious
texts, of abstract imperatives, of (an) absent God(s), at best of

politeness and of love. But why could love not come about in the respect and cultivation of my/our bodies? It seems to me that this dimension of human development is indispensable. Through scorn or forgetting of the body, what remains of it in our traditions is often reduced to elementary needs or to a sexuality worse than animal. To restrict carnal love to a reproductive duty, preceded by elementary coitus, at best by some vague caresses—when the man is not too overwhelmed with work, when one has the time—seems to me, in fact, a degeneration worse than bestial. The majority of animals have erotic displays that we no longer even have. Humiliation—especially of the woman—violence, guilt ... are the lot of most couples in our supposedly evolved civilizations. This is something to be ashamed of! Because this means that love, for us and between us, has become less than human, except for some generous yet rare and often limited exceptions.

The tradition of yoga, the Tantric tradition and certain meetings with spiritual women and men have taught me something different. They have begun to teach me that the body is itself a divine place—the place or temple of the divine in harmony with the universe—or rather they have taught me how to cultivate my body, and to respect that of others, as divine temples. I knew that the body is potentially divine, I knew it notably through my Christian tradition of which it is, in fact, the message, but I did not know how to develop this divinity. Through practicing breathing, through educating my perceptions, through concerning myself continually with cultivating the life of my body, through reading current and ancient texts of the yoga tradition and Tantric texts, I learned what I knew: the body is the site of the incarnation of the divine and I have to treat it as such. That is not always easy, especially in our age, but this makes possible a spiritual becoming that is a lot more stimulating and worthwhile than the perpetual falls and redemptions, inside and outside the flesh, that the majority of the religions of our age teach. The body itself, including in the carnal act, can be deified. That does not mean that it overcomes itself but that it blossoms, becomes more subtly and totally sensible. This transformation, transubstantiation of elementary corporeal matter into spiritual flesh, is achieved particularly through the passage of energy from certain chakras—or psycho-physiological centers—to others: thus from chakras of sexual energy or of elemental vitality to those of the heart, of the throat, of the head, without forgetting the return circulation all the way to the feet. All this alchemy of the becoming of the subtle body is described in certain texts such as the Upanishads of yoga and also in certain Tantric manuals as well as in the teaching of Patanjali on concentration in perception. Everything is not said there, everything is not yet said there as I have sometimes believed. But instructions about the transformations of the body in union with the totality of the universe and about its possible incarnations are given.

The body is then no longer just a more or less fallen vehicle, but the very site where the spiritual to be cultivated resides. The spiritual corresponds to an evolved, transmuted, transfigured corporeal. Music, colors, smells, tastes, singing, carnal love . . . can be of use in this transubstantiation. What I wish to see become from these ancient texts, alas too neglected in our Western(ized) teaching, is that love come to pass between two freedoms.

Often, love is presented there as a union, regressive in a way but ecstatically spiritual, of man with the universal womb that woman would incarnate, chosen as *shakti*. This interpretation is far from being negligible and it is certainly more worthwhile than simple bestial love, rapacious or debased. But the union of two lovers, man and woman, free with respect to genealogy, can realize something other in the incarnation of human love. Each lover, woman or man, can contribute to the rebirth of the other as both human and divine incarnation. In this case, the carnal union becomes a privileged place of individuation and not only of fusion, of regression, or of the abolition of polarities and differences. In love, women and men give back to one another their identity and the potential for life and creation that the difference of identity between them makes possible.

This double identity allows them to remain two in love, and in adult relations of reciprocity.

What Yoga Has Not (Yet?) Taught Me

Our cultural model of love is still most often parental, genealogical, hierarchical. It resembles the teacher-student relationship, the man appearing there as the master and the woman as disciple. In traditions of the goddess, the inverse takes place. It is the man who is initiated into love by the woman.

A PRACTICE OF SEXUAL DIFFERENCE

My wish for the future would be a reciprocal initiation. Which requires that women and men constitute a world proper to their sex or their gender, and that both can offer themselves and can exchange elements of this world other than purely biological ones: sperm and eggs, for example. Men and women have something besides children to engender. I have learned this aspect of spiritual fecundity between the sexes by my own experience and my own desire. When I have tried to explain it—perhaps badly ... —to some practitioners of yoga, it has been poorly understood, even rejected. Nevertheless the practice of yoga continually brings me back to this obvious fact, as do certain texts or commentaries of the Indian tradition. In this way Mircea Eliade often presents the culture of India as a culture that has succeeded in retaining Asiatic aboriginal elements alongside later patriarchal contributions. There is therefore, in India, room for a spiritualization of the masculine and of the feminine. Moreover, it is one of the only traditions where women goddesses and divine loving couples are still venerated.

At the time of a trip to India in January 1984, I was happily surprised to see that the majority of women there, even poor ones, keep a great dignity, an attitude foreign to that of humiliated, submissive, or arrogant women that Western women often have. I am not ignoring what happens in India concerning prostitution, violent acts, and even the murders perpetrated against women. But the one does not prevent the other. There exists there a cohabitation between at least two epochs of History: the one in which women are goddesses, the other in which men exercise a blind power over them.

During this same trip, I was moved when I heard the master T. Krishnamacharya affirm the importance of sexual difference as a dimension of the culture of yoga. That was and still is for me a precious teaching. I would have liked to ask him how to translate the difference of the sexes in practice. It is a question that I still wish to ask yoga teachers, both men and women. I know that there exist practices for pregnant women. But are there practices for women and men inasmuch as they have a different body and spirit? I would like to know them in order to avoid harming my body, in order to develop my qualities as a woman, not only as a mother but also as a lover who is a woman, as a woman philosopher and writer, as a woman speaker, etc.

RECIPROCITY BETWEEN PERSONS

Because of this lack of cultivation of sexual identity, the most irreducible site of reciprocity, reciprocity often seems absent to me in the milieus of yoga. To be sure, a noticeable kindness and a relative respect for the other prevail there. Yet the hierarchical relation often remains what dictates the rules. There also exist few truly spiritual exchanges. For the most part, these are supposed to be useless or even harmful to the practice of yoga. In order to become adept or initiated, it is supposed to be advisable not to think, or to no longer think. This slogan or this ideology, imposed or conveyed in an elementary way by students or teachers of yoga, find attentive and obliging accomplices. Women regularly attend yoga courses in greater numbers; they hear there what they are accustomed to hearing, thus they offer for the most part no resistance. If one among them dares to ask a question that is not agreeable to the teacher, it is quickly made known to her that this question is misplaced and shows a lack of knowledge of what is said or not said in such places. I have lived through this situation several times and I have found it painful and more or less unworthy of practitioners of yoga, who are willing moreover to have truths that are difficult to hear addressed to them by more or less competent masters. Without doubt, it is easier not to think than to think, but the alibi of being a good practitioner cannot prevail against the discipline and the cultivation of the mental. Is practicing without thinking even a part of the tradition of yoga? This tradition seems to me to possess a subtlety that demands, on the contrary, a real aptitude for thought. It is not a matter of thinking any way one pleases. It is necessary to learn again to think without centering on the object, for example, to think in a living and free manner, unattached, neither egological nor possessive. This does not mean not thinking but being capable of going beyond the inertias of thought in order to set its energy free. Is this not the path shown by Buddha and, in our age, in his own way, by Krishnamurti?

THE VALUE OF WOMEN'S VIRGINITY

Both are men. Patanjali is also. Women can certainly learn something from them, while taking care to transmit their own knowledge to men. The majority of spiritual beings attest to this necessity by the need they have of a companion, notably a virgin. It would be worthwhile to make it understood that virginity does not then signify privation or abstention from the realization of the self by a woman subjected to the good will and development of a man, but rather an aptitude of the woman to conserve and cultivate her own identity in order to share its qualities with man in one way or another. This dimension of woman's psychic virginity, kept and cultivated in love and desire with man, is without doubt one of the most extraordinary spiritual riches of humanity, a richness still to be discovered beyond the value of maternity, which is not properly human. If woman does not keep her virginity, she loses her identity and certainly cannot be reborn as a woman. Moreover, becoming simply a mother, woman is no longer a possible companion for man. She is no longer situated on the same genealogical level.

Once again, it is not a matter here of the presence or absence of a physiological hymen, another reduction of sexual difference to simple anatomy, but of maintaining the existence of two sexes, of two genders, as source of biological and cultural creation. It is possible that what paralyzes the becoming of the spirit in our age is the lack of positive tradition concerning the value of woman's virginity. We do not or no longer recognize the value of the virginity of the girl, of the woman for herself and not as exchange money between men, as site of physical engendering of men-heros or gods, as enslavement of the innocence of the woman to the law of spiritual fathers supposedly capable of defining good and evil for all men and all women.

This deficiency of feminine identity transforms the products of masculine intelligence into authoritarian and, in part, artificial, discourses. Men become cultural fathers, and women become natural mothers. The first become the spiritual masters of their mothers. The two sexes, from then on, never communicate between themselves as adults and cannot wed as adults.

I expect yoga to help develop this horizon of the difference of the sexes through taking account of our body and our psyche as women and as men. I fear that practitioners of yoga are moving in the direction of a neutralization of the difference of the sexes, of the treatment of the two sexes "as equals," of the admission of women into the latest and most masculine tradition of yoga while forgetting what they have contributed to it and can contribute to it that is specific to them. If this is how it is, particularly in the Western adaptation of yoga, is it not better most often to renounce such initiations, which are not founded on the reality of bodies and of "souls"?

In fact, women and men risk finding themselves in exile here from their tradition, from their body and from their spirit, without support of a culture that is appropriate to them. It is, in any case, a question that yoga asks: the solitude imposed on the practitioners who walk along this path. This solitude is no doubt increased for Westerners who abandon part of their certainties, conscious or not, in order to entrust themselves to the competence of a practitioner of another tradition. Starting from simple and true realities—the difference of the sexes—seems to me indispensable for reducing the bewilderment and distress that can result from it.

As far as theoretical teaching is concerned, it would seem to me useful to build bridges between cultures: through comparing texts, through encouraging each man and woman to talk about his or her culture in order to attempt to find similarities and differences to share, through listening to the words and writings of those men and women who, in the last century especially, try their best to unite in themselves European traditions and those of the East.

I think that the request of François Lorin concerning what

yoga has given—and not given—me in relation to my European tradition had this intention: to transmit an experience of the way to progress between two traditions, if they really are two.

There remains for me, to be sure, much to say and also much to learn on this subject.

BIBLIOGRAPHY

Desikachar, T. K. V. *Religiousness in Yoga: Lectures on Theory and Practice.* Washington, D.C.: University Press of America, 1980.

Eliade, Mircea. *Patanjali and Yoga.* Trans. Charles Cam Markmann. New York: Schocken, 1969.

— *Techniques de yoga.* Paris: Gallimard, 1975.

Guenther, Herbert V. and Chogyan Trungpa. *The Dawn of Tantra.* Boston: Shambhala, 1975.

Irigaray, Luce. "The Time of Life." This volume.

James, E. O. *The Cult the Mother Goddess: An Archaeological and Documentary Study.* New York: Praeger, 1959.

Lutyens, Mary. *Krishnamurti: The Years of Awakening.* Boston: Shambhala, 1997.

Nayak, Anand. *Tantra, ou, l'éveil de l'énergie.* Paris: du Cerf, 1988.

Silburn, Lilian. *Instant et cause: Le discontinu dans la pensée philosophique de l'Inde.* Paris: J. Vrin, 1995.

— *Kundalini, the Energy of the Depths.* Trans. Jacques Gontier. Albany: State University of New York Press, 1988.

Varenne, Jean. *Les Upanishads du yoga.* Paris: Gallimard, 1974.

The Yoga Sutras of Patanjali. Trans. and commentary by Swami Satchidananda. Yogaville, Va.: Integral Yoga, 1990.

The Way of Breath

Breathing corresponds to the first autonomous gesture of the living human being. To come into the world supposes inhaling and exhaling by oneself. In the uterus, we receive oxygen through the mother's blood. We are not yet autonomous, not yet born.

In fact, we forget this first and last gesture of life. To be sure, we breathe on pain of death. But we breathe badly, and we worry little about the air that surrounds us, our first food of life. We put ourselves under stress in order to force ourselves to breathe: we carry out athletic performances in polluted air, for example. But we do not really take charge of our life, of our respiration, of the air.

We speak of elementary needs like the need to eat and to drink, but not of the need to breathe. That corresponds nevertheless to our first and most radical need. And we are not really born, not really autonomous or living as long as we do not take care, in a conscious and voluntary way, of our breathing.

We remain passive at the level of breathing, bathing in a sort of socio-cultural placenta that passes on to us an already exhaled, already used, not truly pure air.

THE FORGETTING OF BREATH

In the East it is more common to remember that living is equivalent to breathing. And the Sages there care about acquiring a proper life through practicing a conscious breathing. This breathing brings them little by little to a second birth, a birth assumed by oneself, willed by oneself and not only by our parents, and a physiology that dictates its laws to us.

Breathing in a conscious and free manner is equivalent to taking charge of one's life, to accepting solitude through cutting the umbilical cord, to respecting and cultivating life, for oneself and for others.

As long as we do not breathe in an autonomous manner, not only do we live badly but we encroach upon others in order to live. We remain confused with others, forming a sort of mass, a sort of tribe, where each individual has not yet conquered his personal life but lives on a collective social and cultural respiration, on an unconscious breathing of the group, beginning with that of the family.

This breathing remains closer to nature—to the mother, to woman, to the family—or closer to culture—to social or civil life, more tied to the father, to the masculine world in our tradition.

In a way we are divided between two breaths, the natural breath and the cultural breath, without a real alliance or passage between these breaths, neither in us nor between us. Thus we were born and have grown up in the perspective of a separation between corporeal life and spiritual life, the life of the soul, without understanding that the soul corresponds to the life of the body cultivated to the point of acquiring the autonomy and spiritual becoming of the breath.

The culture that we have been taught says that it is necessary to despise the body in order to be spiritual; the body would be the nature that we have to surpass in order to become spirit, in order to become soul. But this culture— contrary to certain cultures of the East, that of yoga for example—does not teach us how to cultivate breathing. Which means teaching us to assure our existence in an autonomous manner and to spiritualize our vital breath little by little while keeping it free, available, nourishing for the body itself, and for others.

Becoming spiritual amounts to transforming our elemental vital breath little by little into a more subtle breath in the service of the heart, of thought, of speech and not only in the service of physiological survival.

Nevertheless, our cultural tradition indicates to us the importance of breathing. Genesis recounts that God created man through sending his breath into matter. And Jesus Christ is born of a woman made fertile by the breath, the Spirit. The most important dimension of our religious tradition is that of the spirit. Christ himself gives way before the Spirit. "If I do not go away from you, the Spirit will not come to you," he says to his disciples. He also asserts that all sins deserve forgiveness, including those against the son of Man, but not those against the Spirit.

The spirit is thus the most important divine dimension. For us, as for the yogis, breathing is what can make us spiritual. But we have forgotten this. And often we confuse cultivation with the learning of words, of knowledges, of competencies, of abilities. We live without breath, without remembering that to be cultivated amounts to being able to breathe, not only in order to survive but in order to become breath, spirit.

The forgetting of breathing in our tradition is almost universal. And it has led to a separation in us between the vital
breath and the divine breath, between body and soul. *yes*
Between breath, that which gives life, and the body, that
which permits keeping it, incarnating it. The union of the
two representing life itself.

This mistaken division between body and soul is, moreover, reflected in our conception of the difference of the
sexes. Woman would be the body, of which man would be
the spirit; woman would represent natural life and man spiritual life. He would even be, in the couple, the representative
of divine life, of Christ as the head. "Women, obey your husband as the Church obeys Christ," writes Saint Paul.

Vital breath and spiritual breath would thus be separated,
and both would be thrown back upon death. Vital breath
returns to inanimate matter if it is not cultivated: what does
not have spirit dies more quickly. But the culture made of
words that no longer bear breath conveys a dead spirit, and
not a living spirit. Without a cultivation of breathing, in each
person and between them, man and woman are also thrown
back upon death. And they remain in a perpetual conflict
concerning who, of the two, best assures the survival of the
human species.

Assuring this survival does not mean only to conceive and
engender children but implies preserving human life as a life

endowed with consciousness, with soul. Now this task belongs to woman as well as to man. It is not the woman's task to bring bodies into the world that man, beginning with the father, will educate. Together man and woman should engender children who are both natural and spiritual.

The event of the Annunciation, which marks the passage from the Old to the New Testament, reminds us of this. What has been said of it has often been a little naively puritanical and not very spiritual. And the theologians have been quite materialistic in looking for the proof of Mary's virginity in her physiological hymen. Mary is a virgin because she was able to keep and to cultivate a spiritual relation to breathing, to the soul. It is not at the level of the bodily hymen that we should interpret the mystery of the Annunciation. The conception of a divine child depends on the quality of breathing and on the exchange of words that precede it—on its announcement.[1]

Mary, the Tradition teaches us, would atone for Eve's offense. I understand the message in this way: Eve wants above all to know, which includes knowing things that have a relation to the divine. Now God cannot be reduced to knowledge. Wanting to appropriate knowledge of the divine, Eve consumes a breath that is irreducible to knowledge. Conserving her virginal breath, free and available, Mary retains a relation to life, to the soul, to love, particularly divine love, that is neither appropriation nor consumption of the self, nor of the other, nor of God.

THE MOTHER'S SILENT TEACHING

It is impossible to appropriate breath or air. But one can cultivate it, for oneself and for others. Teaching takes place then through compassion. And the same goes for engendering. It is a matter in both cases of giving-sharing one's breath with one who does not yet know the way of natural or spiritual life.

The Eastern master shares his breath, passing on to the disciple a part of the breath that leads him to awakening. This awakening is not conserved in words, it is practiced, it is won at each moment through respiration. The bliss of awakening is thus partially suspended in order to teach, not because of a will for power or authority but because of compassion. In fact, the teaching of the master is what cures suffering and death. Buddha, like Christ, is a doctor before being a professor: he teaches in order to remove suffering, in order to educate others to avoid physical or psychological suffering.

Woman, faithful to herself, is close to Eastern cultures, close to the Buddha, who, moreover venerates the feminine spiritual. Woman shares her breath. Either she remains at the level of vital breath, by giving oxygen to the fetus through

her blood, or she shares spiritual breath, and that, in my opinion, is akin to the meaning of Mary's virginity.

Before feeding, before giving herself as nourishment, woman
gives or, more exactly, shares her breath, her natural and spiritual life. We have not yet understood such a mystery. At the
level of existence and of being, we have forgotten the importance of breathing in human and divine life. And yet this has
been taught to us, in words and in images, in our tradition.
But those who transmit this spiritual testament often transmit
it as dogmas or truths of the past and not as gestures to be
made by us here and now.

Woman, like the creator God, engenders with her breath.
But she does it from the inside, without demonstration. She
does it invisibly and silently, before any perceptible word or
gesture. Woman teaches, through her very doing, at each
moment of the present and in a continuous manner. Through
carrying the child, through speaking to the child, more generally through mothering the child once born, she shares her
life, her breath. If she gave it without keeping some of it,
without remaining alive, the other would lose existence. She
does not simply give, she shares. But what she shares is not
seen.

The example given to explain the meaning of the word
symbol is an object cut in two of which each takes and keeps

a part. Here, there is no object and no division in two: the symbolic economy is much more subtle.

If I have spoken of breath at the level of maternity, it is because maternity is often spiritually valorized as material gift, of blood, of body, of milk, and not as sharing of breath, sharing of life, sharing of soul.

The mother gives her breath and lets the other go; she gives the other life and autonomy. From the beginning, she passes on physical and metaphysical existence to the other.

We are accustomed to praising the mother for more or less ambiguous reasons: the need to reproduce the species, the need to produce citizens, the necessity for man to give himself descendants and also the respect, even worship, of what would be a sacrificial gift on the part of woman, a gift of herself, one says, and not a sharing of life and breath.

AWAKENED BY DESIRE

Woman as woman, the female lover are more often scorned than praised, at least on the spiritual level. They are the guardians of the body, of nature, necessary, to be sure, but who constantly put the spirit at risk. They are an occasion for seduction but also for degeneration. We have few women spiritual masters in the West. In the East, the woman has long been the first and even the sole sexual and spiritual initiator. Sometimes the two initiations have hardly been distinguished. And, if we reflect a little, this is not as naive or diabolical as one may believe. Desire is often awakened by the woman. Now desire is *something more* with respect to need. It is probably specifically human. The animal perhaps does not desire; it feels a sexual excitation that it satisfies, including an excitation to reproduce. Human desire is more complex; it is always in part spiritual, even if the body, considered by us to be purely natural, is its place. We understand human sexual attraction poorly because it is tied to the invisible and to the imperceptible of the flesh: to the soul, to the breath.

Unless we are being perverse, necrophilous, in desire we look for *something more* of life; we hope for a supplement of life from the other. Already, desire itself awakens us to a life generally asleep in us. To desire really represents an awakening. But we do not know how to cultivate this awakening. Instead of making energy rise or descend in us, between the centers (the chakras, one says in the Eastern tradition) of elemental vitality and the more spiritual centers, we think of desiring someone (man or woman), rather than a sort of spiritual mystery hidden in that someone. We want to possess the other as an object instead of approaching the other in order to share

with him or her the energy of desire, between desiring and
desirable subjects.

Sexual desire has generally been taught to us as a work of
the flesh alone and not of the spirit. This error has paralyzed
the energy of man and of woman in the Western tradition. It
has also made us regress to animality, to instinctual attraction,
including that of procreation. It has made sex an instrument
of possession, of perversion, of death, instead of finding in
sexual difference a spiritual path, which can lead us to love, to
thought, to the divine.

Genesis teaches that sin would be wanting to know all,
wanting to appropriate divine knowledge, instead of respecting it as breath. It is not sexual energy that is sin, but its paral-
ysis in knowledge, techniques, and the will for possession or
for power.

As such, sexual desire is awakened to the spiritual, in oneself and in the other. It meets with two failures: the reduction
to knowledge or the regression to simple nature. These two
impasses represent the dichotomy, to be overcome in our tradition, between body and spirit, between woman and man.

In order for this to happen, it is important to recognize in
each person a proper body and spirit instead of cutting
human being in two: half man, half woman.

The human species is made up of two genders, irreducibly
different, attracted to one another by the mystery that they

represent for each other, an undisclosable mystery that is a source of natural and spiritual life.

What attracts man and woman to one another is not a simple sexual instinct, which could be satisfied by a passage to the act. We are regressing today to this stage because sexuality has become what is at stake in a commerce subjected to diverse speculations and techniques. We also regress to this stage because man and woman forget the mystery of their difference, they reduce it to a corporeal particularity useful for the production of an orgasm and of a child.

What is at stake in the attraction between the sexes thus disappears. All sorts of stimulants and drugs become necessary in order to arouse desire, a desire that will retain its hunger because it does not involve the entire being.

SHARED BREATH

In fact, what attracts man and woman to each other, beyond a simple corporeal difference, is a difference of subjectivity, and notably a difference of relation to the breath.

It is the vitality or the soul of a woman that attracts a man, as much as and more than a sex or a beauty already artificially formed. The most beautiful girls are not always the most desirable, except on television or in film. What the boy looks for in the girl is a supplement or a path of life. And, if desire as such—not love—often goes from the man toward the woman, it is that the woman has in her a greater reserve of breath. Man uses his energy in order to fabricate, to make, to create outside of himself. He puts his vital or spiritual breath into the things that he produces; he employs it in order to build a world, his world. He keeps little of his breath, his soul, in him. And, in order to maintain it there, he needs instruments: concepts, dogmas, rites, etc. But breath is then no longer free, no longer shareable.

Woman, more spontaneously, keeps breath inside her. It is a question of physiological identity, and a question of relational identity as well. Born of a woman, her mother, with the capacity to engender and to love like her, the little girl possesses from the beginning, within herself, the secret of human being and of the relation between human beings.

The little girl is born with familiarity to self, to the natural world, to the other. She intuitively knows the origin of life. She knows that the source of life is in her, that she need not construct it outside of herself. Her breath need not leave her in order to build, to fabricate, to create. It needs, on the contrary, to remain in her to be able to be shared, to be made fertile. Woman also remains in greater harmony with the cosmos. This allows her to inhale and to exhale more naturally that which nourishes the vital breath: air.

To separate himself from the mother, the origin of his life, the boy, the man, builds for himself a world different than the cosmic universe, a world that is in some way artificial. The same is true at the level of vital breath and at the level of spiritual breath: God in the masculine is further away from micro- and macrocosmic nature than a feminine divinity.

The little girl, the woman, breathes in order to live but also in order to share, to communicate, to commune. It is true on the natural plane, and it should be this way on the spiritual plane.

But, by subjecting woman to masculine spirituality, our tradition has taken her soul away from her and has thus deprived man of a spiritual resource, including a resource in carnal love. If the carnal act can appear to him as a little death, it is because he forgets what he can receive that is spiritual through drawing near to the breathing of woman. The same is true if it appears to him as a "sin," as an offense. To be sure, this spiritual to which he draws near is not the same as his own. It sometimes remains simple breath, without words, without rites, without visible transformation of air, of energy. But if this breath is situated at the level of the center (of the chakra) of the heart, of speech, of listening—as in the Annunciation— this breath is pure spiritual being. It corresponds to what the masters of the East look for, as well as certain Western mystics who take the negative way in order to join the divine as

God—nothing (*nada*), nothing but breath having passed from the level of elemental vitality to the spiritual level.

Love, including carnal love, can become this mystical negative way. In love, each person renounces all solitary pleasure, including representative pleasure, and uses desire for the becoming of energy in the relation, for the transformation of sexual attraction into love, into speech, into thought without, however, annihilating it. This is not to say that the two become one, but that each follows a specific path so that the relation is possible in the moment and in the long term, despite or thanks to the difference between the two.

WOMAN AS SPIRITUAL GUIDE

So woman has, from her birth, an almost spontaneous taste for relational life, which probably comes to her from the fact of being born of someone the same as her, with whom she can moreover identify in love and in generation. Woman searches for the relation to the other, where man searches for the relation to the object. The risk, for woman, is that she effaces herself because of the attraction for the other. In every sexual relation, in the sexual relation strictly speaking, woman will need to make an effort to safeguard the two of the intersubjective relation. She must not give herself up in love or desire for the other, which would mean annihilating the two.

She must not any longer reduce the other to a same as oneself, or to a child, which would correspond to a form of repetition of the first relation that she knew with her mother. She must maintain the two, and maintain it outside of a principally natural relation, such as generation. The girl knows a relation to the other almost by nature: that with her mother, that with the child. The relation to man, unless it demeans this relation, obliges her to pass beyond the almost natural intersubjectivity tied to reproduction.

The first relation with the other that woman knows is a relation linked to respect for and the sharing of life: the life that her mother respected so that she could be born and survive, the life that she herself respects in becoming a mother. The highest spirituality for woman does not reside there, even if the sharing of life as such is already a gesture that mythologies and even religions formulated in the masculine have not taught us. Our culture is full of stories of fathers who kill their sons or sons who kill their fathers, of fathers who rape their daughters and get them pregnant. Thus ethics often appears, for man, to come down to respect for the life of the other, particularly in the genealogical relation.

For woman, the ethical gesture begins with respect for the spiritual life, and not only the natural life, of the other. What man claims as ethics, woman realizes almost involuntarily on a daily basis: to not kill the one who brought you into the world nor the one whom you will engender. The awakening of consciousness, for a woman, is situated at a spiritually higher level: not only to not destroy the life of the other, but to respect his or her spiritual life and, often, to awaken the other to a spiritual life that he or she does not yet know.

The relational life of man is paralyzed by the difficulty of entering into relation with the one who gave birth to him. To overcome such a difficulty, religions have often devised a physiological virginity in the mothers of spiritual men: Buddha or Jesus for example. An anti- or counternatural mystery would allow giving birth to a son not paralyzed by a natural attraction for the mother. As for philosophy, it invented the split between matter and spirit, sensible and intelligible, etc.

The way to resolve the question is different. Despite being rational, perceptible, and practicable by all men and women, it has been neglected. It is the *spiritual* virginity of woman that can help man to discover relational life. A corporeal relation with the other gender that does not come down to a natural relation, to a regression to simple nature, to breathing for survival, allows man to attain a relational life made of both body and spirit.

The role of woman as lover is in some way superior and more inclusive compared with that of the mother. She makes the breath of man pass from natural vitality or from fabricating energy to interior life: a life tied to the centers—or chakras— of the heart, of speech, of listening, of thought.

Carnal love becomes thus a spiritual path for energy, the flesh becomes spirit and soul thanks to the body itself, loved and respected in its difference, including at the level of breathing.

Sexual difference is, in fact, the difference that can open a transcendental horizon between humans, in particular between man and woman. The transcendence that is revealed and worked out in this manner, in the respect for each person's natural and spiritual life, is more radical than that relating to genealogy. Transcendences, masculine as well as feminine, tied to genealogy are both too dependent on the natural world and too fabricated. They divide us between natural life and divine life without our being able to ensure the passage from the one to the other at each moment. It is in sexual difference that the split between human and divine identities can be overcome, thanks to a cultivation of energy, in particular a cultivation of breathing. Between man and woman, thanks to love, including carnal love, an awakening to transcendence can take place that corresponds to the reign of spirit as spiritual breath, as soul. A soul not localized and enclosed, as the masculine soul is, but a soul that progressively animates the whole body, changing its inert materiality or its elemental vitality into spiritual existence through a transmutation of energy.

This passage to another epoch of the reign of spirit depends upon a cultivation of respiration, a cultivation of breathing in and by women. They are the ones who can share with the other, in particular with man, natural life and spiritual or divine life, if they are capable of transforming their vital breath into spiritual breath. This task is great, yet passionate and beautiful. It is indispensable for the liberation of women themselves and, more generally, for a culture of life and of love. It requires patience, perseverance, faithfulness to self and to the other. Women are often lacking these virtues today. But why not acquire them? Out of love of self, out of love for the other? Out of consciousness of the importance of women's spiritual role for the present and the future of humanity.

Being I, Being We

We find ourselves today faced with a new situation with regard to culture: we are witnessing a growth of information in space as well as in time, an accumulation of knowledge on diverse levels and, at the same time, a loss of human consciousness. We know more things but we return less to ourselves in order to examine the meaning of all these things for a more accomplished human becoming. We are discovering that many realities have remained unknown to us up until now but the discoveries that we are making are so numerous that we forget somewhat the reality and the limits of our own being. And the risk exists of knowing a thousand things, of finally reducing ourselves to an effect of acquisition of knowledge, but of no longer knowing anything about who *I* am, who *you* are, who *we* are. The risk exists that we are becoming computer software with a multitude of stored programs but for which the key for defining the possible unity of these programs is missing, as is the manner of passing from one program to the other, the means of using the whole or a part of it in order to communicate with ourself, with the other, between us.

THE WAYWARDNESS OF WESTERN CONSCIOUSNESS

Such a crisis of culture is tied to a certain conception of being conscious, at the level of the *I* and at the level of the *we*. In Western culture the subject is constituted by moving away from the/its naturalness through conflicts, the use of tools, and control. This natural belonging can present itself in the form of corporeal birth, genealogical relations with the mother or sexual relations with the loving partner; it can also exist in the form of individual or collective relations with the cosmic environment. To become conscious means dominating this immediate mode of perceiving, this immersion in a world not constructed by the I. To become a subject involves turning away from the pre-given natural milieu in order to create a universe of one's own thanks to bodily or technological instruments among which language appears as a privileged tool.

Now this turning away from life and from natural wisdom—if I can express myself in this manner—entails unforeseen consequences with which we are confronted today. For example, a cultural production and information that does not allow us to return to ourselves, to have our feet on the ground, and to keep a present and living relation with the other, with others, a relation that is not already mediated by an abstract and neuter universal, at least in appearance.

The risk of a loss of consciousness exists for three principal reasons. The first results from the unorganized multiplicity of information that overwhelms us and in the face of which our intellectual or spiritual salvation demands passing to a universal level without ensuring the necessary mediations of such a gesture. Another danger comes from the fact that man has tried to dominate nature through various instruments or tools, but instead now finds himself in large part dominated by these instruments and the products made thanks to them. In this way we are today surrounded by a technical universe that reduces each of us to an "I"—or better, to any old "one" as Jean-Paul Sartre writes—any old "I" that obeys the imperatives of the used object or of the constructed milieu in which we live. All this promotes neither the development of a living consciousness for each of us nor the sharing of a common life: we live isolated from one another by an already made world, obeying the orders of objects and of the universe that surrounds us. It suffices, for example, to watch the film *Modern Times* again, and to understand that we are all, men and women, at the service of technical chains that impose their laws on us, and not just in our place of work. Which constitutes a third reason for the current crisis of the subject as well as that of the community.

We risk thus losing ourselves in our own productions and forgetting finally the reason for which we produced them: to dominate nature. Moreover, in a certain way, nature no longer exists and what helped us to emerge as human consciousness has disappeared. We live in a created world, a second world, that no longer corresponds to the natural universe in relation to which man defined himself as subject: as *I* and as *we*. Noting that, in this second world, the concept of human nature no longer has much to do with our natural identity shows us that it is already a matter of an artificial and abstract naturalness. Deprived of such reference, we oscillate between an abstraction without anchorage in our own nature and a regression to animality. For a significant number of individuals, families, and human groups the animal is again becoming the totem, and animality the model of functioning for the *I* and for the *we*.

The human species thus seems to be searching for its way between an objective but abstract construction in which it is alienated from itself (whether it is a matter of the universe of technique, of the socio-political ideology of equality without differences, of a medical competence founded on the knowledge of human cadavers or of other living species, or of a competition between human intelligence and computer programs) and a regression to animal instinctiveness or to corporeal inertia.

The extent of this oscillation is ever greater, for individuals as well as for human groups, torn between imperatives henceforth exterior to themselves, thus manipulated by more or less visible and human masters, and a return to the familiarity or the complicity of the animal world. And it will be difficult to overcome the gap between such polarities in a new figure of History, particularly because they no longer resemble those of the dialectic we know: living consciousness on one side, unaccomplished objectivity on the other.

THE INSURMOUNTABLE MEDIATION OF GENDER

But there exists a third way that permits the pursuit of human becoming while opening a new epoch of History. This way, it is true, obliges us to change our traditional manner of reasoning. But changing methods is better than losing consciousness. It is a matter of renouncing the attempt to constitute consciousness through a domination of nature: cosmic universe, naturalness of the mother or of woman, origin of life or of instinct. It is a matter of abandoning a path of knowledge that is autarchical, abstract, and not really objective and of interpreting Western consciousness, the Western subject, our "being I" and our "being we," as subjected to mediations proper to the masculine subject, and thus not really universal or neutral. It is then discovered that nature as human nature is *two*: masculine and feminine, and that it requires a double subjectivity, a double "being I," in order to be cultivated.

Such a path for the becoming of consciousness is without doubt the most civilized and the most spiritual that presents itself to us today. It joins together empirical necessities and transcendental necessities. It binds, in fact, in a new dialectical relation, nature and culture, making of the difference of nature—of gender, of age, of race, for example—a difference insurmountable by an absolute consciousness. In this way the objectivity of an unsurpassable difference will always be opposed to the domination of a consciousness. This consciousness will remain tied to nature, to concrete singularity, that is to say that it will remain incarnated, escaping abstract universality.

The most universal and irreducible difference, from this point of view, is the one that exists between the genders. It appears as the empirical as well as transcendental condition for guaranteeing the possibility of a new epoch of History or, more simply, for assuring for humanity a becoming. Indeed, it imposes a difference on consciousness, and one that is insurmountable, thus a becoming without end. Moreover, this difference corresponds to a difference between living consciousnesses, and the risk of enclosing consciousness in an erroneous objectivity, in a fictitious and dead absolute, is reduced, as is the risk of confining oneself to an instinctive animality. It is not the same thing to have as a partner in the dialectical movement and process a more or less inanimate, more or less proper objectivity to surpass or to reach, or a subjectivity that obeys different necessities than my own. In the latter case, the dialectic becomes, or becomes again, dialogue between two consciousnesses; it thus returns to a real relational process and is not content with a method of domination on the part of one consciousness in relation to nature, to natural immediacy: that exterior to oneself, that in oneself or that between us.

From then on, the becoming of consciousness, of culture, cannot be entrusted to one subject alone; it is engendered in the interaction between two subjectivities irreducible to one another: that of man and that of woman. Thus there no longer exists one sole logos, defined always and forever in the horizon of only one absolute or only one God, and supposedly inscribed in the neurons of the human species.

There are two linguistic chains that enter into interaction, leaving open the totality of meaning and of its verbal, gestural, or plastic expressions. Between these two subjects, man and woman, there takes place then not only a natural generation, that is to say children, but also a spiritual generation, a culture foreign to a unique objective and a unique absolute. There is no risk, thus, of a totalitarian order imposed by only one truth, only one subjectivity, only one leader.

A NEW TASK FOR HISTORY

At a time when it is possible to think that humanity has accomplished its becoming, exhausted its capacities and its memory, the existence of a double subjectivity opens a horizon yet unknown for our History. And it would be helpful from now on to abandon the cross of suffering entailed in a realization of the absolute—to cite the words of Hegel—an absolute saturated with language, in order to return to the absolute silence that the respect for other as irreducible to oneself calls for.

Negativity is then applied to the absolute itself as the accomplishment of the subject, an absolute reduced not to nothing but to a silence attentive to the other. The way of negative theology—perhaps imagined by humble Beguines before its use in the discourse of the mystic of the Rhine—should be followed today by all philosophers, men and women, in order to be in accord with the truth of "being I" and of "being we." Would it not be, in fact, in the construction of a truth unknown to the self alone, of a truth to share with others, to share between us, that the subject would accomplish its becoming, in the consciousness of an absolute limit—that of the other—which allows each of us to return subjectively to our self in order to cultivate a proper and singular interiority? Each of us no longer resembles a hunter of the absolute at war with every other but becomes the humble builder of a human interiority.

The most recent Western philosophers have asked themselves the question of the end of philosophy, of the return to self or to the origin of our culture, of the horizon of death as condition of consciousness. They have not imagined that the limit sought for by them could be found in the fact that consciousness is two, that it can and should be defined with respect for the other as irreducible to oneself. Nor have they sensed that such a discovery could represent the possibility of a new epoch of philosophy and even of ontology, but an ontology founded on "being two."

Obviously, we then find ourselves before a radically different "being I" and "being we." In order to realize them, the first objectivity that we should care about is not science, nor religion, nor even art, objectivities that—according to

Hegel—can testify to an accomplished subjectivity, but rather the mediation of a law that guarantees the identity of persons in their singularity. Such a legislation will have for its task protecting, thanks to an objective guardianship, the difference between subjects, particularly the difference of gender. The mediation of law would be the universal code for the institution of a symbolic world that does not perpetuate an ethical offense toward the feminine "I" and "we," that is to say that guarantees an equivalence of laws for the two genders, while respecting their difference(s). That would allow each citizen to become and to cultivate himself or herself, on the condition of respecting the cultivation of the other sex.

In such a perspective, neither the *I* nor the *we* can be structured starting from a still unrecognized and uncultivated instinct that cements a unity dominated by the concept. The "being I" and the "being we" are constituted starting from a consciousness of the self as limited, from an individual or collective responsibility that does not efface the singularity of each person. Difference is not preserved by a vertical transcendence, but thanks to the horizontal transcendence of the other gender as irreducible to me, to mine.

Community is then composed of autonomous individuals in conscious relation to one another. It does not come down to an undifferentiated whole of citizens organized by an instinct, a will, an idea, or a leader, whether it be the leader of a horde, of a tribe, of Church or of State. In fact, such a leader resembles the patriarch who assures the unity of a family founded on an already artificial naturalness. In this family unit, each member, the man, the woman, or the children, alienates his or her own singularity in order to form a whole of which the side called natural will remain "private," subtracted from the civil community, and the side called "cultural" or conceptual will become public, visible, and will be governed by a male citizen or, in the best of cases, a so-called neuter citizen.

Changing the "being I" and the relation between "being I" and "being we" requires modifying this family organization, refounding the family on a joint contract between two different subjects, a man and a woman, who decide, with regard to themselves and the community, to assure this unit of transition between the "being I" and the "being we" that we call the couple.

In reality, a society composed as a being-in-relation, and not as an entity dominated by a leader, is made up of an infinite number of couples who should continually assure between them the passage from instinct to culture in the respect for the proper nature of each one. It seems to me that constructing a more accomplished human community cannot be realized in a different manner. Likewise, to constitute it according to a democratic ideal is impossible without renouncing the all-powerful genealogical order, always founded on a hierarchy, in favor of horizontal relations between subjects. The relation between the genders seems the privileged place for the creation of horizontal relations, whether these relations are realized in private life or public life, between adults or between children.

The "being I" and the "being we" will thus be modified. They will from now on be constituted and cultivated as "being(s)-in-relation," concerning the individual as well as the social group. The relations will remain concrete, at the empirical and transcendental level, and they will unite the necessities of the moment and those of eternity, without sacrificing any singularity, and while respecting the exigencies of a temporal constitution.

Such would be one of the mysteries of a love respectful of difference: to intuit or to glimpse an absolute ideal without claiming to realize it objectively or alone. Leaving it in its condition as a star that lights up a path opened together and that should be pursued in faithfulness to a yesterday, a today, and a tomorrow, provided that this faithfulness is not a renunciation of the singularity of each "I" and of each "you."

The Family Begins with Two

Recently, in the context of a colloquium, I was explaining the necessity of refounding the family on a more conscious and more civil alliance between man and woman. A man intervened, saying that the family began with three and not with two. I am not in agreement with such a position. In my opinion, a family is born when two persons, most generally a man and a woman, decide to live together on a long-term basis, to "set up a home," to recover an old expression that, deep down, is beautiful.

To start a home and family is to set up a new dwelling, a new house, in particular around a center, often likened to the domestic hearth: a place that is used for eating, for warming oneself, for gathering. It was this way in ancient Greece; the mother carried a flame from her own hearth in order to light the domestic fire of her newly married daughter.

In reality, the family is not founded on three, but on two. To make it begin with three is to reduce it to that undifferentiated unity described by Hegel, a unity in which the man, the woman, and the child or children lose or alienate their own identity in a whole cemented by naturalness, but an already abstract and neuter naturalness that erases the physical, psychological, or legal singularity of each person.

In this type of family organization, the commitment made between an adult man and woman to live together on a long-term basis, in mutual respect, becomes blurred in the face of the subjection of the man, the woman, and the child to the necessities of natural reproduction, itself subjected to the imperatives of the reproduction of society, of the State.

In this case the family no longer represents a privileged place of love and spirituality but a more or less unified whole, dominated by procreation, genealogy or filiation, parental authority, particularly paternal authority, and the possession of goods.

THE DECLINE OF THE FAMILY ORDER

Such a family order is now in crisis, and its organization does not resist the culture of our age. From all sides, families are exploding: mother on one side, father on the other, children who come and go between them. This breaking down of family unity leads to pain, confusion, despair: for everyone, parents and children. Symptoms of repression also appear, as if it sufficed to intervene with a little authority in order to reestablish a past stability, and why not a traditional number of children.

This solution appears at once impractical, ineffective, and undesirable. In fact, the chances of a future for humanity exist in moving away from belonging to the animal world toward the conquest of a more accomplished human identity. The possibilities of a future for the human species do not reside in a return to a simple natural identity, neither for the individual nor for the family, and even less so because the family obeys socio-cultural imperatives that have already perverted the relation of each person to a singular nature. The family, then, is founded on a lack of real education about sexuality for each person, desire being left or maintained there at the level of instinct and/or perversity, both of them justified by a parental abnegation in the service of the State and, in a different way, of religious communities.

Such a socio-cultural organization supposes a human immaturity, framed by habits and rites related to those of the animal world, including the behaviors that we consider to be the mark of an accomplished generosity.

Such an order also implies a system of rules and norms defined outside of the relation between man and woman, rules and norms that the legislative and executive powers of the State, and, in a different way, of Churches, take the liberty of decreeing and sanctioning even in the most intimate aspects of the carnal relation, preventing this relation from being lived between the two. The relation between two would be forbidden without the intervention of a third: of a natural, religious, or civil nature.

Does this imperative of the presence of a third mean that the relation between two does not yet exist? Or does it have for its goal the prevention of its coming to pass?

And why appeal to human or divine law of obligation or of prohibition where this relation is trying to find itself or is coming about? To remind humans that they are humans? Why, in this case, in the name of the most physical aspect of the flesh: reproduction? In the name of what is also going to confuse the two with one, reducing to a single flesh—already abstract unless it is that of the child—the bodies and the desires of those who love each other: man and woman?

All that does not seem a good sign for the human family, reduced in this way to a reproductive tribe subjected to the authority of a father-head.

Many no longer want this authority.

First the women who refuse henceforth to be considered as

a simple reproductive ground, who demand the right to speech, to desire, to liberty, to the "soul." This does not mean that they no longer want children, but that they want to be able to say "yes" to engendering in themselves, that they want children born of flesh and speech, and not according to the traditional modality where the mother remains the body impregnated by the spirit of the father. Women want to co-create with man through body and speech, and not only to passively and silently welcome the masculine seed, whether it be material or spiritual. Women lay claim to deciding, in the name of their nature to be sure, but also in the name of their spiritual abilities. They refuse to be subjected to paternal or marital order, be it private or public. This chapter of patriarchal history seems to be disappearing, whatever the current regressions or convulsions. The work of women's liberation movements certainly contributes to its passing, but the psychoanalytic culture as well, which, while it still expresses itself too often in terms of patriarchal laws, makes the individual consciousness of the woman grow, inciting her not to accept as destiny suffering, privation of joy, the reduction to corporeal and affective passivity.

Children also criticize paternal authority. And, if they have not yet discovered a guaranteed way for a new becoming, they refuse nevertheless to bow to the old patriarchal rules and norms. At best, parents are tolerated by them as friends, as confidants.

The time of the father's sacred authority appears past. To be sure, we are witnessing heightened movements of regression—as is happening with women—and requests for an absolute authority. Times of transition are subjected to oscillations where the best and the worst can appear: for example, a beginning of a cultural revolution can be followed by a formalistic repression more terrible than that which preceded the insurrection.

The authority of the father is thus challenged, in the family strictly speaking but also in diverse forms of political or cultural families. And it is not with patriarchal repression that the family will be saved or restored. Nor does the return to matriarchy seem the best solution, even if it is generally accompanied by a less abstract relation to the natural world.

FROM NATURAL IDENTITY TO CIVIL IDENTITY

There exists a third way that is newer and more in accordance with human becoming: to refound the family, not on parental authority, paternal or maternal, but on the love between woman and man, man and woman.

Before taking the time to reflect, some men or women will say that it has always been like this. But this is not true. Years ago, the hand of the daughter was granted to the suitor by the father, and the man accepted the daughter as wife on the condition that this choice was accompanied by a dowry, whether it be a matter of money, of real estate or lands, of name, etc. The love between those engaged was thus subjected to patriarchal rites, which considered it not as an adult engagement between a man and a woman but as the occasion of a contractual alliance between families, possible thanks to certain conditions.

There remain numerous traces of this historical stage, notably in legislation. Thus, in France, the legal age of marriage is eighteen for a boy and fifteen for a girl, in other words the age of civil majority for the one and the age of natural maturity for the other. Not yet of age, a girl needs parental consent if the marriage is to be valid; she thus passes in some manner from the authority of the father to that of the husband without first attaining civil majority as a woman. Another example characteristic of the majority of the most evolved civil codes: the sharing of parental authority between the father and the mother is legally recent. And it is in the neuter or in the masculine—as "breadwinner"—that the woman can exercise it, and not as a woman.

There is not yet a civil identity in the feminine. One of the symptoms of such a deficiency is that the State and religious communities have the power to legislate upon the body of the woman, on her pregnancies for example.

Another sign: seduction or violence toward the woman, toward the feminine body, always appears as a social fact, a customary right as it were, on the subject of which the State and the Churches generally remain silent. Woman still seems a private or collective good over which the father, the husband, the citizen have rights without the interested party having her say. And, according to certain penal codes, it is supposedly only toward his conscience, or toward God, that the man would be guilty if he sexually assaulted a woman, but not toward her. How could she herself be offended? She does not exist as civil person. She is a body-nature that is available to masculine sexual instinct, to the desire or need for a child, etc.

Sometimes this body-nature cries, cries out, claws or bites, really or symbolically, but that does not yet amount to becoming a civil person. Certain men and women attempt to console her, to heal her, with private or public advantages, with kind or pleasing words. But that does not transform her into a civil person.

In order to attain the status of civil person, woman must pass from natural identity, especially an imposed natural identity, to civil identity. Her most radical and indispensable (r)evolution is situated there. It is not only a matter, for her, of criticizing the patriarchal world, of asserting herself outside of it, other than it. She cannot limit herself to becoming conscious of this historical universe in order to pass beyond its horizon. She must become aware of herself as woman. The task is extremely difficult. Whoever has long remained reduced to a

natural identity or to a slave consciousness cannot give themselves overnight a consciousness of their own. Taking charge
of one's own nature, giving it positively an end, a goal, an ori-
entation, a "soul," does not happen in one day.

And, if the diverse movements of women's liberation have
accomplished extraordinary things in several years, they have
not for all that reached this stage. A certain group of women
generally limits itself to critique, to opposition, to the constitution of a world parallel to the masculine world; another
group contents itself with obtaining equality with men, in particular through the acquisition of social advantages. Both have
often affirmed a difference solely at the affective, subjective
level without asking for or constructing an objective dimension that assures them an identity of their own and allows them
an alliance with the other half of the sky and the earth.

To this civilly autonomous feminine becoming, the State
and religious communities are often opposed, but so are
women themselves. They often remain at the age of puberty
or prepuberty, in opposition to the adult world of today,
which they imitate and reject at the same time, without
attaining a real human maturity. They can give birth, to be
sure, but there is nothing particularly human about that. They
nurture, certainly, but a child or an adolescent can do that.
And the same goes for keeping house. The sign of human
maturity for woman would be to remain woman without

being subjected to the masculine world or to her own nature. It would be a matter, for her, of escaping from the simple submission to nature without for all that renouncing it: being able to choose love, being able to choose motherhood.

CARNAL SHARING AS SPIRITUAL PATH

That seems simple in words. In fact, such choices do not go without saying. It is complicated to remain autonomous in desire without wounding the desiring, the desired, or the desirable. That necessitates the construction of an interiority that is still lacking for us. This interiority may represent for women access to a transcendence of their own. It implies respecting the other and respecting oneself while assuring bridges between two irreducible worlds.

If such a task is entrusted only to natural identity, to reproduction, to the parental function, the union between man and woman does not reach human maturity, and the singular identity of each one disappears in the family unity. A family then represents a horizontal link of an institutional organization in the present, and a vertical link in genealogical ascendance or descendance and the development of History. The family does not correspond to the place of accomplishment of human maturity. It remains a more or less animal tribe.

The path for realizing human identity would be found, not

in the renunciation of carnal love, in a privative chastity, but rather in a carnal sharing capable of passing beyond instinct—including at the level of procreation—appropriation, possession; a carnal sharing also capable of going beyond the regression or disappearance of consciousness in a return to a so-called natural order that ignores all difference and all transcendence.

Carnal sharing becomes then a spiritual path, a poetic and also mystical path, a path of chastity in a more rigorous sense than a pure and simple renunciation of the flesh that is not yet a renunciation of its fantasies, of its illusory or ideological productions, that often abolish the dimension of intersubjectivity.

Carnal sharing becomes the discovery of a measure, an experience of the realization of self in the consciousness of a limit, and of a complicity with the other to respect. Love comes about with two, thanks to opening to the other as other, to his or her irreducible being, thanks to the renunciation of being the whole all by oneself. Love takes place in the opening to self that is the place of welcoming the transcendence of the other. In this case, there is nothing of a fall or lapse; it is rather elevation, Jacob's ladder, transubstantiation or transfiguration of the flesh.

The path of such an accomplishment of the flesh does not correspond to a solipsistic dream of Luce Irigaray, nor to a fin-de-siècle utopia, but to a new stage to be realized by humanity. It alone seems to be able to refound the family in the direction of a historical progress that manifests itself both as a more real democracy at the political level and, at the religious level, as a new "sacramental" union—even if it is celebrated only by a civil marriage—that those who love each other confer on themselves, a conjugal "sacrament" that has no reason to envy the priesthood, a more social and collective ministry than marriage is.

At a time when sexuality has lost part of its secrets and taboos, to make of carnal sharing a spiritual way, a way of "salvation" for solitary desire, opens a beautiful horizon for a refoundation of the family. It becomes the place not of a repression or of an exploitation of the flesh but of a poetic, even mystical, progression of love, a path of renunciation of absolute love of oneself with a view to carry out love with the other in the giving up of both self and other, emotionally as well as intellectually. Sexuality no longer contents itself with blind perversion, with nihilistic seduction, or with the production of a more or less abstract energy; it does not claim to dominate or to subjugate through a technique. It becomes abandonment to the opening of self and other toward wisdom still unknown.

Everything thus finds itself modified: the mode of perceiving, of touching, of speaking. Everything takes place and is carried out by two, in the respect for the other whose irreducibility is transformed into a mystery that illuminates.

Nature then is no longer subdued but it is adapted, in its

rhythms and necessities, to the path of its becoming, of its growth. Caressing loses the sense of capturing, bewitching, appropriating that this gesture keeps in the discourse of certain recent masculine philosophers: Sartre, Merleau-Ponty, and even Levinas, for example. The caress becomes a tactile word, which recalls that we are two, *I* and *you*, which awakens each one to self and to other, which invites abandoning the clarity of judgment in order to rejoin a more nocturnal light, that of sensibility, that of the flesh, that of the soul perhaps. Caressing is no longer limited to being a maternal consolation, an alleviation of suffering, nor does it invite falling back into infancy, animality, bodily unconsciousness. The caress becomes a means of growing together toward a human maturity that is not confused with an intellectual competence, with the possession of property—among them the bodies of the beloved and of the children—nor with the domination of the world, beginning with the little world of the house, of the family. Love, including carnal love, becomes the construction of a new human identity through that basic unit of the community: the relation between man and woman.

BECOMING PARENTS, BECOMING CITIZENS

Engendering will happen of its own accord when the overabundance of love wants fruits other than the becoming of man and of woman. But generation ought not be imposed as an a priori limit of love on pain of mutilating the identity of the man, of the woman, and of the child.

It does not seem that a possible future for the family is found in its natural character considered as "sacred," as John-Paul II has again written recently to all the heads of state, on the occasion of the Cairo Conference, invoking, in order to support his words, article 16(3) of the Universal Declaration of Human Rights affirming that the family is "the natural and fundamental element of society."[1] Such words seem to be the inheritance of a rather naive paganism, and they annul the development of History, particularly Christian history.

It is not the reduction of the family to its natural dimension that can assure it a future but a cultivation of the union between man and woman in the respect for their differences, which implies that nature becomes consciousness. In order to be and to remain two in love, including carnal love, it is necessary, in fact, that the body become flesh awakened by consciousness. It is necessary that the man and the woman enjoy an equivalent dignity and that they discover together how to combine nature and spirituality across their differences of body and subjectivity.

There is no doubt that, if they carry out their union in this way, man and woman will become citizens prepared for the democratic sharing of community life: they have in effect already crossed over the most difficult stage to reach there.

Such a loving journey will also lead the man and the woman to acquire a possible parental identity. The horizontal coexistence between the sexes, the most necessary coexistence, the most desirable but also the most difficult to realize, leads naturally and spiritually to the respect of ancestors and to hospitality toward future generations. But it is not appropriate to impose as imperatives or obstacles *before* what will come to pass on its own *after.*

The first and principal task in order to found or refound a family resides in the work of love between a man and a woman, a woman and a man, who, in the name of desire, intend to live together for the long term, to combine, in them and between them, the moment of the birth of attraction with the perpetuation of love, the instant with eternity.

BIBLIOGRAPHY

Irigaray, Luce. *Democracy Begins Between Two*. New York: Routledge, 2001.
— *An Ethics of Sexual Difference*. Trans. Carolyn Burke and Gillian C. Gill. Ithaca: Cornell University Press, 1993.
— *I Love to You*. Trans. Alison Martin. New York: Routledge, 1995.
— *To Be Two*. Trans. Monique Rhodes. New York: Routledge, 2001.
— "Transcendants l'un à l'autre." In Xavier Lacroix, ed., *Homme et femme, l'insaisissable différence*. Paris: du Cerf, 1993.

Approaching the Other as Other

We have been educated to make our own all that was pleasing to us, all that we admitted into our proximity, into our intimacy, all that surrounded us.

On the level of consciousness, on the level of feelings, we make our own what we approach, what approaches us.

Our manner of reasoning, even our manner of loving, corresponds to an appropriation. Our culture, our school education, our cultural formation want it this way: to learn, to know, is to make one's own through instruments of knowledge capable, we believe, of seizing, of taking, of dominating all of reality, all that exists, all that we perceive, and beyond.

We want to have the entire world in our head, sometimes

the entire world in our heart. We do not see that this gesture transforms the life of the world into something finished, dead, because the world thus loses its own life, a life always foreign to us, exterior to us, other than us.

Thus, if we precisely grasped all that makes the springtime, we would without doubt lose the wondrous contemplation in the face of the mystery of springtime growth, we would lose the life, the vitality, in which this universal renewal has us participate without our being able to know or control where the joy, the force, the desire that animate us come from. If we could analyze each element of energy that reaches us in the explosion of spring, we would lose the global state that we experience by bathing in it through all our senses, our whole body, our whole soul.

We sometimes, at least partially, find this state again, I would say this state of grace, in which the spring puts us, when we are immersed in a new landscape, in an extraordinary cosmic manifestation, when we bathe in an environment that is simultaneously perceptible and imperceptible, knowable and unknowable, visible and invisible to us. We are then situated in a milieu, in an event that escape our control, our know-how, our inventiveness, our imagination. And our response to this "mystery" is or could be astonishment, wonder, praise, sometimes questioning, but not reproduction, repetition, control, appropriation.

THE IRREDUCIBLE TRANSCENDENCE OF THE YOU

The state that springtime, certain landscapes, and certain cosmic phenomena provoke in us, sometimes takes place at the beginning of an encounter with the other.

It is in the first moments of drawing near to one another that the other moves us the most, touching us in a global, unknowable, uncontrollable manner. Then, too often, we make the other our own—through knowledge, sensibility, culture. Entering our horizon, our world, the other loses the strangeness of his or her appeal. The presence of the other included us in a certain mystery, communicating to us an awakening that is both corporeal and spiritual. But we reduce the other to ourselves, we incorporate the other in turn: through our knowledge, our affection, our customs. At the limit, we no longer see the other, we no longer hear the other, we no longer perceive the other. The other is a part of us. Unless we reject the other.

The other is inside *or* outside, not inside *and* outside, being part of our interiority while remaining exterior, foreign, other to us. Awakening us, by their very alterity, their mystery, by the in-finite that they still represent for us. It is when we do not know the other, or when we accept that the other remains unknowable to us, that the other illuminates us in some way, but with a light that enlightens us without our being able to comprehend it, to analyze it, to make it ours. The totality of the other, like that of springtime, like that of the surrounding world sometimes, touches us beyond all knowledge, all judgment, all reduction to ourselves, to our own, to what is in some manner proper to us. In somewhat learned terms, I would say that the other, the other as other, remains beyond all that we can predicate of him or her. The other is never this or that that we attribute to him or her. It is insofar as the other escapes all judgment on our part that he or she emerges as *you*, always other and nonappropriable by *I*.

To recognize the *you* as irreducible to us, unknowable and imperceptible by us in his or her totality, is not our habit. Our culture has generally entrusted this *you* to God, what is more, to God-the-Father. Our habits of thought, our ethical or political habits toward the other who is present to us or with us here and now—carnally, bodily—go rather in the direction of reducing the other to ourselves, to our own, or of transforming the other into a *he*, sometimes into a *she*, in some way reduced to an "object" of knowledge or an "object" of love.

In this way, never without doubt has an age spoken so much of the other as ours does, globalization and migrations requiring it. But, too often, this other is reduced to an object of study, to what is at stake in diverse socio-political strategies aiming in some manner to integrate the other into us, into our world. Thus we avoid the problem of meeting with the stranger, with the other. We avoid letting ourselves be moved, questioned, modified, enriched by the other as such. We do not look for a way for a cohabitation or a coexistence between subjects of different but equivalent worth. We flee dialogue with a *you* irreducible to us, with the man or woman who will never be *I*, nor *me*, nor *mine*. And who, for this very reason, can be a *you*, someone with whom I exchange without reducing *him* or *her* to myself, or reducing *myself* to *him* or *her*.

The transcendence of the *you* as other is not yet, really, part of our culture. At best, the other is respected in the name of tolerance, is loved in God, is recognized as an equal or a fellow human. But that does not yet amount to perceiving and respecting the irreducibility of the other, to recognizing the irreducible difference of the other in relation to me.

This letting go of the subject, this letting be of the *I* toward what it is, knows, and has made its own, this opening of a world of one's own, experienced as familiar, in order to welcome the stranger, while remaining oneself and letting the stranger be other, do not correspond to our mental habits, to our Western logic. Dominating, controlling has been taught to us as the realm of reason more than accepting our limits, in order to live together, to coexist, to co-create even, with who or what exceeds us, extends beyond us, remains irreducibly exterior and foreign to us.

We have learned to think starting from a certain number of dichotomies between sensible and intelligible, nature and spirit, body and soul, subject and object, etc. And we do not know how to transform such categories in order to attain a culture of alterity, of relation with the other as such, of acknowledgment of the other as irreducible to us, in order to make an alliance with him, or with her, in the respect for our respective values and limits.

At best, we are sometimes good patriarchs or good matriarchs. But this genealogical behavior, implying nature and hierarchy, still avoids the meeting with the other: the man or woman that I must horizontally recognize as equivalent to me, in the radical respect of his or her difference(s).

Two events of our time compel us to rethink our relation to the other as other: 1. the blending of races and ethnicities that is now a part of our daily landscape, 2. the recognition of the importance of gender from a cultural point of view. One could add here a certain coexistence of generations that does not allow genealogy to retain its past function.

In fact, we are entering a new age of generalized mixing, and our mental or community habits founded on self-identity, the proper, the similar, the same, the equal, and their reproduction, risk being incapable of harmoniously resolving the problems of difference that we have to manage.

To make the Black equal to the White, the woman equal to the man, is still to submit them, under cover of paternalist generosity, to models put in place by Western man, who resists living together with the different. He even accepts becoming a little Black or a little female rather than going through a revolution of thinking that is today unavoidable. All the strategies of integration—with more or fewer reversals of hierarchy, blendings and pluralities of culture, of language, of identity— yes, but not the gesture that recognizes that the subject only exists thanks to limits and that, before the universe and especially before the other, the subject is structured not by mastering or dominating but by accepting that the subject is not the whole, that the subject represents only one part of reality and of truth, that the other is forever a *not I, nor me, nor mine*, and not a: *not yet I, not yet mine* to integrate into me or into us.

SEXUAL DIFFERENCE, THE FOUNDATION OF ALTERITY

For this revolution of thought, of ethics, of politics, of which we have to take charge today, sexual difference represents the most interesting question.

First, this difference is universal, and it allows us, as such, to define a model of global community.

Next, it is often the manner of treating this difference—in the sexual relation or in the genealogical relation—that is at the origin of differences of tradition, of culture, manifesting itself notably in common law. To find it a democratic regulation would help the coexistence of cultures.

Moreover, this difference is the one that can bring together the most natural with the most cultural, by requiring us to take a new step in the construction of a civilization.

In fact, in our cultures, woman still often remains the natural pole of a masculine culture. If each gender assumes, in itself and for itself, the specificity of its nature and works out its cultivation, a new type of civility will be put in place in which the duality of the genders will become, thanks to their differences, culturally fertile, and not only naturally fertile as it still is too exclusively today.

To refound society and culture upon sexual difference is also to radically put back in question the notion of the proper, of propriety, of appropriation that governs our mental and social habits. It is to learn, at the most intimate, at the most passionate and carnal level of the relation to the other, to renounce all possession, all appropriation, in order to respect, in the relation, two subjects, without ever reducing one to the other.

To affirm that man and woman are really two different subjects does not amount for all that to sending them back to a biological destiny, to a simple natural belonging. Man and woman are *culturally* different. And it is good that it is so: this corresponds to a different construction of their subjectivity. The subjectivity of man and that of woman are structured starting from a *relational identity* specific to each one, a relational identity that is held between nature and culture, and that assures a bridge starting from which it is possible to pass from one to the other while respecting them both.

This specific relational identity, one's own relational identity (the word is used now in another sense, not of possession but of subjective or objective determination), is based on different irreducible givens: the woman is born of a woman, of someone of her gender, the man is born of someone from another gender than himself; the woman can engender in herself like her mother, the man engenders outside of himself; the woman can nourish with her body, the man nourishes thanks to his work; the woman can engender in herself the masculine and the feminine, the man, in fact, intervenes as man above all in the engendering of the masculine.

The first relational situation is thus very different for the girl and the boy. And they build their relation to the other in a very different way. The girl immediately finds herself in a relation between subjects of the same gender that helps her to structure a relation to the other, which is more difficult for the boy to develop. On the other hand, the girl, the woman is made fragile by the intervention of the other in her: in love, in motherhood.

The construction of subjectivity for the woman implies that she comes out of an exclusive relation with the same as herself, the mother, and that she discovers the relation with a different other, while remaining herself. Egalitarian or separatist strategies cannot resolve such a problem. What can assist the woman in becoming subject is the discovery of the other, the masculine, as horizontally transcendent, and not vertically transcendent, to her. It is not the submission to the law of a Father that can permit the woman to become herself, corporeally and culturally, but the conscious and voluntary recognition, in love and in civility, of the other as other. This cultural becoming of the woman will then be able to help the man to become man, and not only master and father of the world, as he has too often been in History.

It seems that the woman must give birth to the man not only bodily but also spiritually. Certain religious traditions have sometimes clearly expressed this reality.

The assimilation or integration of the feminine into the masculine world represents therefore a real danger for private or collective relational life. That does not mean that the woman must remain the guardian of love in the traditional sense, but that she must be the one who initiates relational life and who safeguards it in private and public life.

Mixing: A Principle for Refounding Community

Not so long ago, the founding of a home was a matter of alliance between properties, between names, between common laws. The girl and the boy were given permission to leave the paternal house on condition of perpetuating the patrimony, the titles, the customs. Leaving one's home, yes, but in order to remain among ourselves.

Marriage was supposed to preserve wealth from all deterioration, customs from all change. Nothing foreign was supposed to alter the intimacy constructed between those of the same group, passed on by the ancestors. The principle task of future spouses came down to bequeathing the heritage to their children. The goal of the family was in fact to guard possessions and to make them proliferate: personal belongings, real estate, cultural and human possessions. This is how it carried out its role toward a society of which it assured a fundamental permanence, authorizing in this way a more secondary historical evolution.

THE FAMILY IS NO LONGER WHAT IT WAS!

European unanimity on the fact that the family must remain sacrosanct continues to go in this direction. The same goes for the indignant appeal to the inviolability of private life invoked against the request of rights for persons passing into the very interior of a family's unity: rights for women and children, for example.[1]

Is this not wanting to blind oneself to what is already taking place? The family unit has been, for some time, subjected to transformations that have changed its conditions. When it survives, it is at the price of mutations that have modified its meaning. The composition of a natural entity, propped up by legal institutionalization, functions partially now as ideology. There are diverse reasons for this. The faithfulness to just one common law is possible these days only in certain sectors of society, and yet . . . Wealth and possessions? They seem to have somewhat deserted the family monopoly to become the privilege of industrialists, bankers, and other big businessmen, such as States. The authority of ancestors? Does it not find itself weakened by the rights of love and desire? Not to mention the transformation of ideals, the "fall of idols."

In short, this fixed base of a traditional society, the family, only survives because of mutations that reshape its norms and values. An example of this might be a couple constituted by a woman and a man of various traditions, even races, surrounded by children, part natural, part adopted, living without economic or geographic stability, in a more or less nomadic and multicultural manner.

Institutions evolve less quickly than reality! And this gap is particularly evident today. It is true that the change has been rapid, and it can be understood that citizens and administrators find themselves somewhat disconcerted by this. Does not the sacrosanct place of safeguarding customs resemble a miniature international site under construction? Is not that which should assure the permanence of the same crossed these days by differences foreign to our customs and our knowledge? Has not the overturning of tradition invaded the very heart of what assured its durability?

The evolution is so abrupt and unforeseen that the most regressive orders seem to want to cover it with a veil or suffocate the evidence of its reality. And, instead of asking how to treat this fundamental socio-cultural innovation, we often worry about diverse forms of integration that sterilize its potentials rather than promoting its fertility.

Looking closely at this, do we not find ourselves faced with laboratories where, in miniature, the historical becoming of humanity is worked out? Cultural elements that children would have learned with difficulty all year long at school are offered to them at home, or with friends, as bits of daily life. If, from the youngest age, diversity is admitted and respected, the child will learn a second language, will familiarize himself or herself with more than one tradition, will be brought up with tolerance toward the stranger.

While public authorities will look into the difficult problem of integration, new families will have initiated the young generations into a cohabitation that is multiracial, multicultural, etc. Does not wanting to integrate mean, in effect, claiming to reduce diversity to a unique model, already obsolete in reality? If the family is the resisting nucleus of social construction, has it not already said "no" to this standardization imposed from above? Has it not already chosen difference as a springboard for survival?

TO INTEGRATE OR TO COEXIST?

Curiously, that which imposes itself upon us in this age, both from the top and from the bottom, still finds itself frustrated by administrative, legal, and political habits that refuse to be put into question. It is true that this compels a revolution in the way of thinking, the necessity of which few realize. Of which few are able? Except children? And those who desire?

But the evident contradictions of the current world require changing the principles that govern it. The growing entropy of our socio-cultural organizations necessitates the passage to another order. It is not possible, for example, to advocate abandoning national sovereignty for the needs of the construction of the European Union and to claim, elsewhere, to integrate immigrants into a nation. Such inconsistencies come to confront one another sooner or later; which does not contribute to the development, nor even to the maintenance, of a civil community.

How then to treat the problem of the blending that has swept through a Western tradition founded on the logic of identity to self, of the same, of the similar, of the equal?

Rather than turning to norms incapable of finding a solution for new conditions, it is preferable to question the resources of the situation and to discover a possible positive structuring of them.

Thus, a couple formed by a white woman and a black man can, from the fact of its being multiracial, become a site of civic education for the surpassing of instinct, be it innate or acquired, but it can also regress to the level of a human instinctuality by cutting itself off from the surrounding society, which is perceived as rejecting, incapable of recognizing it as such. Recognition cannot mean reducing the two to the same. If difference has nourished desire, why not respect it?

In fact, all attraction is founded upon a difference, an "unknown" of the desiring subject, beginning with what pushes the boy and the girl, the man and the woman toward each other. Would not the conviviality between citizens be better if it involved discussing our taste for what differs from the self? Why exclude from the composition of the unity of society this leavening agent of connection?

To be sure, society has need of a minimum of shared rules. But they are not impossible to discover.

Civil community is based on the family entity, this in its turn being founded upon the union of man and woman. The duality of the sexes cuts across all races, all cultures, all traditions. It is therefore possible to organize a society starting from this difference. It presents the double advantage of being globally shared and of being able to join together the most elemental aspect of the natural with the most spiritual aspect of the cultural.

I am not referring here to a bad use of sexual difference, which leaves woman the guardian of the natural pole in a unity of which man secures the cultural pole. I am thinking of a relation between the sexes in which woman and man each have a different subjectivity, based notably on both a relational identity of their own and a relation to language of their own.[2]

If the desire between woman and man comes to accord with a civil status, while respecting the difference(s) between them, the relation between the genders can serve as a relational paradigm for the refoundation of a family in the strict sense and, more generally, for a mixed society, in all senses of the term. Managing to respect the other of sexual difference, without reducing the two to the one, to the same, to the similar . . . represents a universal way for attaining the respect of other differences.

A LEGISLATION OF NEW DESIGN

But the appeal to great sentiments is not enough for passing from the respect reserved for the same to respect toward the other. Something must change in the way of thinking, which escapes simple good will. The modifications to carry out are, moreover, multiple and complex. And the rhythm at which they can be fulfilled differs from one individual to another, from one socio-cultural sector to another.

It is a question therefore of defining an objective framework thanks to which such mutations can be realized without destructuring civil community. This historical evolution seems to be capable of taking place in a peaceful and fruitful manner starting from the formulation of additional legislation guaranteeing the rights of persons as such.

The current French Civil Code deals above all with guarantees relative to the property of citizens, the body itself forming part of the register of a "good" the protection of which the State ought to assure. While saying much about relations to property, the law has not been very explicit about its role as regards the defense of the identity and the dignity of citizens, of their access to the symbolic world, of the relations between them. All these aspects of citizenship, which do not come directly under the realm of "having" but have more of a relation to "being," are still largely unknown to our lawmakers. While they are sometimes perceived when it is a matter of intervening in the territory of others, as testified by certain articles of the Charter of Human Rights, they seem to remain ignored when we are implicated. And we are ready to confuse the other with ourselves, notably inside our borders, in order to not question our legal codes, in order to not approach the irreducible core of the human being, which mixing requires us to consider outside of our cultural customs.

The generalized mixing in our age puts before us two possible strategies: either to go further in the reduction of the other to the same, or to recognize difference as a fundamental character of the living. The first way leads us to a neutralizing reduction that borders on the ghostly; it corresponds, unfortunately, to our customs, particularly our legal ones. The second way brings us to a consistency, including a carnal consistency, that calls for a new cultural elaboration. We are still lacking a culture of between-sexes, of between-races, of between-traditions, etc. Globalization has never been as concretely present to us, but the subjective and objective means to assume this historical reality are still to be worked out.

The gathering together of men and women who until now lived far away from one another, unknown to one another, leads to better realizing the complexity of human identity, the multiplicity of its subjective facets, its relational aspirations and difficulties, its need for objective contexts in order to develop individually and to live together in peace.

In this global coexistence, we are discovering a particularly evident fact: the conception of our traditional culture needs to be rethought. The West has founded the rational on the domination of the natural world. Belonging to a human nature is conceived here as a necessary evil that it is important to transform into abstract categories as soon as possible: linguistic rules, philosophical concepts, scientific criteria, legal norms, religious dogmas, etc. It is by distancing itself from a sensibility still linked to nature that human subjectivity is thought to be cultivated at the social level. Poets, mystics, women, children, "savages" would remain marginalized under the supervision of a dominating world unacquainted with the corporeal, with affect, with the living as such. From this perspective, all that evokes nature must be restricted, educated, distorted by neuter uses that reduce its singularities.

CHASE AWAY THE NATURAL, IT RETURNS AT A GALLOP

This conception of reality and of its possible elaboration in the world cannot withstand the coming of the global, including its coming among us. A nature, irreducible to our customs and to our restrictions, reappears everywhere, and challenges us to welcome it democratically.

How to do this without taking into consideration differences of age, of sex, differences of race, not to mention their diverse symbolic constructions, varying from one culture to another? There is no lack of work if we are to avoid, in this, all authoritarianism, all totalitarianism! All the more so since it implies the changing of mentalities. Where we have learned to control nature, it would be a matter of learning to respect it. Where the ideal has been presented to us as the absorption of the whole in an absolute, it would be a matter of recognizing the merit of insurmountable limits. Where respect for the same stretched, vertically, from the son to the Father-God and, horizontally, to the universal community of men, it would be important from now on to know how to intertwine love of the same and love of the other, faithfulness to self and becoming with the other, a safeguard of the identical and the similar for the meeting with the different.

It is a new agenda, for which we lack the training. Cultural fertility would no longer be tied to the improvement of a single subject in relation, whether as accomplice or rival, with its peers. It would result from listening and the effects of mixing, difference revealing itself there as a source, not only of natural fertility between man and woman, but also of spiritual and symbolic productions the novel character of which would be proportional to the situations with which we are confronted daily.

The most interesting situation is probably that of families where diverse types of blending [*mixité*] intersect. The resistance to belonging to a natural identity appears there in the horizontal axis that joins the sexes and in the vertical axis that links together generations. These two axes appear as the only universals, and are thus able to restore in their economy the dimension of race.

Paradoxically, these fundamental coordinates come up against obstacles that are their symbolic by-products. Common law, in effect, comes down for the most part to rules concerning customs in relations between the sexes and between generations. The variations between these rules may be explained by nonhomogeneous relations of subordination of one tradition to the other. Discovering an order not founded on subjection, for a democratic coexistence in mixing, would offer a way of approaching problems of cultural mixing.

If the woman and the man are considered as individuals of equivalent dignity and worth, some differences in customary and legal norms can find a common platform. For example, the differences between marriage codes most often express variable degrees of oppression of the woman by the man, whether it be a matter of the legal age of marriage, of access to property for each spouse, of respective parental status, or of polygamy, of the right to divorce the spouse, of sexual norms ranging from the obligation imposed upon the woman to follow her husband to the most atrocious bodily mutilations.

The right to cultural and legal identity for each of the two sexes can solve such divergences that indicate degrees of slavery or emancipation more than real diversities. Rethinking the irreducible components of masculine identity and of feminine identity in their aspects that are liable to a legal formulation is necessary as a preliminary step for acceding to a generalized mixing. The task is not impossible. It suffices to be attentive to the contents of the demands that are voiced from certain quarters in order to understand that they come down to rights to objectively decree and enforce laws. For women, the operation is particularly necessary because they are emerging from an age-old patriarchal tutelage that leaves them without legal identity, particularly in the family context.

THE KEY ROLE OF MIXED FAMILIES

But the human individual cannot be reduced to an economic entity, and the efforts of our societies toward a greater equality between the sexes at this level, apart from the fact that they are insufficient and sometimes more virtual than real, do not exhaust the legislative needs of women: the right to human dignity, including dignity in the sexual domain in the strict sense, the right to the free and responsible choice of maternity, the right to a valorizing language, religion, culture, etc.

These rights, relative to the civil protection of a specifically feminine "being," are still lacking. The family unit, conceived as a whole in which the man, the woman, and the children give up their legal singularity in order to form a unity founded on an exclusively natural blending [*mixité*], is, to a great extent, the cause of this. But it is also, today, the reason for an evolution. Besides the refusal of a good number of women to secure the undifferentiated natural pole in the couple, the family, or society, cultural blending [*mixité*] reinforces the need for legal self-rule by each member of a family in which natural identity is sometimes complex and diversely taken over by cultural belonging.

In order for mixing not to become a cause of regression but a factor of progress, it is fitting to protect it against all instinct of possession, of submission, against all residue of animality in the human. The generalized diversity of our age must push for the creation of links between nature and culture that a simple sexual difference did not seem to require. Marriage between a white woman and a black man, between a Catholic woman and a Muslim man, will either become an extraordinary seed for growth for our civilizations, or it will lead to instinctual resurgences absent from our traditions, privileging customs in which the power of some over others emerges more virulently than in our own. Unless it brings about a still more imperious submission of individuals to economic transactions that neutralize human specificity?

From this point of view, mixed families represent a key place for the construction of our future societies. They will then either testify to a decline of human consciousness, to an economic fate that leaves us in a cultural ill-being and impotence, or they will participate in a more or less tranquil world revolution. The demands of crossed blending [*mixité*] disturb our mental habits, our common laws, our legislative criteria.

They compel us to transformations of desire, of thinking, to civil forms of meeting and cohesion of which we have hardly an idea.

How thus to realize them? By refusing to subject the respect of the other to the assertion of the same, the present or future to the past. By accepting that the development of a civilization does not inevitably consist of the accumulation of goods, of products, of knowledge inside an unchanged horizon. Some ages demand the change of the horizon itself. This is true of our age. We have to let go of our models of identity founded upon equality or similarity if we are to put ourselves to the test of differences that require rights that are equivalent but not reducible to the same, to the equal, to the one. Political agendas, like educational ones, need new formations, perspectives, words, and logics in order not to take the ideals of the past for progressive generosity.

This fin de siècle, if it does not mark the entry into another era, risks being nothing but a pitiful decline of the human species . . .

NOTES

THE TIME OF LIFE

1. Arthur Schopenhauer, *The World as Will and Representation*, trans. E. F. Payne, vol. 2 (New York: Dover, 1966).

2. See on this subject Mircea Eliade, *Patañjali and Yoga*, trans. Charles Lam Markmann (New York: Schocken, 1969).

In India the Indo-European cultures have not destroyed or covered over the Asiatic aboriginal cultures. Numerous prepatriarchal cultural elements, closer to a feminine tradition, thus survive despite the Aryan contributions privileging the reign of the father and the characteristics of patriarchal economy.

To meditate on physical gestures, in particular the cosmic respiration of the Buddha, rather than on the logical subtleties of a Buddhist discourse, to speak of incarnations of Brahma and of his acts at the limit of the mortal and the immortal, the human, the divine, and the elementary is, as far as

I am concerned, a deliberate choice which is careful to respect aboriginal cultures. The same goes for the utilization of the term *Hindu*.

In effect, the term *Hinduism* is often used to designate "the religious victory of the soil" (cf. Mircea Eliade, ibid., p. 176), namely, the forms of subsistence of pre-Aryan aboriginal traditions.

3. Cf. Lilian Silburn, *Instant et cause: Le discontinu dans la pensée philosophique de L'Inde* (Paris: J.Vrin, 1955, rpt., De Boccard, 1989).

THE WAY OF BREATH

1. On this subject see Luce Irigaray, *I Love to You*, trans. Alison Martin (New York: Routledge, 1995).

THE FAMILY BEGINS WITH TWO

1. "Acts of Pope John-Paul II," *Osservatore Romano*, April 8, 1994, French translation in *Catholic Documentation*, May 15, 1994.

MIXING: A PRINCIPLE FOR REFOUNDING COMMUNITY

1. See on this subject Luce Irigaray, "The Family Begins with Two" (included in the present volume, first published in French in the journal *Panoramiques: La famille malgré tout* [1996], no. 25); *Sexes and Genealogies*, trans. Gillian C. Gill (New York: Columbia University Press, 1993); *Je, tu, nous: Toward a Culture of Difference*, trans. Alison Martin (New York: Routledge, 1993); and *I Love to You*, trans. Alison Martin (New York: Routledge, 1995).

2. See on this subject Luce Irigaray, *I Love to You*, and "Homme et femme, une identité relationnelle différente," in *La place des femmes* (La Découverte, 1995).

EUROPEAN PERSPECTIVES

A Series in Social Thought and Cultural Criticism
Lawrence D. Kritzman, Editor